DR. ABU AMEENAH BILAL PHILIPS

تفسير سورة الملك

Tafsīr 67

A COMMENTARY ON SURAH AL-MULK

ISBN 978-1-898649-73-1

British Library Cataloguing in Publication Data.
A catalogue record for this book is available from the British Library.

Published & distributed by

Al-Hidaayah Publishing & Distribution Ltd

PO Box 3332, Birmingham B10 0UH, United Kingdom.
T: 0121 753 1889 : F: 0121 753 2422
E-mail: mail@al-hidaayah.co.uk : www.al-hidaayah.co.uk

TABLE OF CONTENTS

QUR'ĀN: THE UNIQUE BOOK*

The word "Qur'ān," a verbal noun, is equivalent in meaning to "*qirā'ah*," as both come from the verb "*qara'a*" which means "to read." That is, Qur'ān literally means "a reading or reciting."[1] However, the term "Qur'ān" has been historically used specifically to refer to the book which was revealed to the Prophet (ﷺ). The term "Qur'ān" is mentioned in a number of places throughout the Book in reference to itself. For example:

إِنَّ هَٰذَا ٱلْقُرْءَانَ يَهْدِى لِلَّتِى هِىَ أَقْوَمُ

"Verily, this Qur'ān guides (man) to that which is most just."
Sūrah al-Isrā' (17):9.

* This introduction is taken from *Usool at-Tafseer*, pp. 85-113.

[1] *Arabic-English Lexicon*, vol. 2, p. 2502.

The name Qur'ān is used to refer to both the Qur'ān as a whole, as in the previously quoted verse; as well as to each verse or group of verses, as in the following verse:

وَإِذَا قُرِئَ ٱلْقُرْءَانُ فَٱسْتَمِعُوا۟ لَهُۥ وَأَنصِتُوا۟ لَعَلَّكُمْ تُرْحَمُونَ ﴿٢٠٤﴾

"And, if the Qur'ān is recited, you should listen to it quietly (and be silent)."
Sūrah al-A'rāf (7):204.

The Book has also been referred to by other names; for example, the *Furqān* (The Distinction):

تَبَارَكَ ٱلَّذِى نَزَّلَ ٱلْفُرْقَانَ عَلَىٰ عَبْدِهِۦ لِيَكُونَ لِلْعَٰلَمِينَ نَذِيرًا

"Blessed is He who revealed the Furqān to His slave in order that he may be a warner to all the worlds."
Sūrah al-Furqān (25):204.

and the *Dhikr*, (The Reminder):

إِنَّا نَحْنُ نَزَّلْنَا ٱلذِّكْرَ وَإِنَّا لَهُۥ لَحَٰفِظُونَ ﴿٩﴾

"Verily, We revealed the Dhikr and verily We will preserve it."
Sūrah al-Ḥijr (15):9.

The Qur'ān could be defined as Allāh's words which were revealed in Arabic in a rhythmical form to Prophet Muḥammad (ﷺ). Its recitation is used in acts of worship and its smallest chapter (*sūrah*) is of a miraculous nature.

The Prophet's divinely inspired statements which were recorded by his followers are generally referred to as *ḥadīths*. For example, the Prophet's companion (*ṣaḥābī*), 'Umar ibn al-Khaṭṭāb, reported that he once said,

إِنَّمَا الأَعْمَالُ بِالنِّيَّاتِ

"Verily, deeds are (judged) by their intentions."[2]

However, in some of his statements, the Prophet (ﷺ) attributed what he said to Allāh; for example, another *ṣaḥābī*, Abū Hurayrah, reported that the Prophet (ﷺ) said,

يَقُولُ اللهُ عَزَّ وَجَلَّ: أَنَا عِنْدَ ظَنِّ عَبْدِي بِي . وَأَنَا مَعَهُ حِينَ يَذْكُرُنِي . إِنْ ذَكَرَنِي فِي نَفْسِهِ، ذَكَرْتُهُ فِي نَفْسِي . وَإِنْ ذَكَرَنِي فِي مَلأٍ، ذَكَرْتُهُ فِي مَلأٍ هُمْ خَيْرٌ مِنْهُمْ

"Allāh, Most High, says, 'I am as My slave thinks of Me and I am with him when he remembers me. So if he remembers Me to himself, I will remember him to Myself and if he remembers Me in a group, I will remember him in a better group.'"[3]

In order to distinguish this type of *ḥadīth* from the previous type, it is referred to as *ḥadīth qudsī* (holy *ḥadīth*) and the former is referred to as *ḥadīth nabawī* (prophetic *ḥadīth*).

The Qur'ān, however, is not the same as *ḥadīth qudsī* for a number of reasons. First, the Qur'ān is from Allāh both in its wording and in its meaning, while in the case of *ḥadīth qudsī*, its meaning is from Allāh but its wording was the Prophet's (ﷺ). Second, Allāh challenged the Arabs and mankind in general to produce even a chapter equivalent to one of the Qur'ān's chapters, and their inability to do so proves its

---

[2] *Sahih al-Bukhari*, vol. 1, p. 1, no. 1; and *Sahih Muslim*, vol. 3, p. 1056, no. 4692.

[3] *Sahih al-Bukhari*, vol. 9, pp. 369-70, no. 502; and *Sahih Muslim*, vol. 4, p. 1408, no. 6471.

miraculous nature. This is not so in the case of *ḥadīth qudsī*. Third, the recitation of the Qur'ān is used in *ṣalāh* and is itself considered a form of worship. The Prophet (ﷺ) said,

مَنْ قَرَأَ حَرْفًا مِنْ كِتَابِ اللهِ فَلَهُ بِهِ حَسَنَةٌ وَالْحَسَنَةُ بِعَشْرِ أَمْثَالِهَا لَا أَقُولُ
آلم حَرْفٌ، وَلَكِنْ أَلِفٌ حَرْفٌ وَلَامٌ حَرْفٌ وَمِيمٌ حَرْفٌ

> *"Whoever reads a letter from Allāh, Most High's Book, will get a good deed (recorded for him), and each good deed is worth ten times its value. I am not only saying that Alif Lām Mīm is a letter, but I am also saying that Alif is a letter, Lām is a letter, and Mīm is a letter."*[4]

However, the recitation of *ḥadīth qudsī* carries none of these properties.[5]

The Mode of Presentation

The Qur'ān is God's final communication of His divine will to humankind. It is the Creator speaking to human beings and it takes the form of human conversation. As humans change subjects randomly during conversation, the topics of the Qur'ān change in a seemingly random way. Consequently, the format of the Qur'ān is quite unique among books.

The Main Theme

Not only is the Qur'ān unique among books today in its origin and purity, but it is also unique in the way it presents its subject matter. It is not a book in the usual sense of the word

---

[4] Reported by Ibn Mas'ūd and collected by al-Tirmidhī and Aḥmad; and authenticated in *Ṣaḥīḥ Sunan al-Tirmidhī*, vol. 3, p. 9, no. 2327. See *Riyād al-Sāliheen*, vol. 2, p. 512, no. 999 for the English version.

[5] See *Principles of Islamic Jurisprudence*, p. 15, and *Qawā'id al-Taḥdīth min Funūn Muṣṭalaḥ al-Ḥadīth*, p. 56.

wherein there is an introduction, explanation of the subject, followed by a conclusion. Neither is it restricted to only a presentation of historical events, problems of philosophy, facts of science or social laws, though all may be found woven together in it without any apparent connection or link. Subjects are introduced without background information, historical events are not presented in chronological order, new topics sometimes crop up in the middle of another for no apparent reason, and the speaker and those spoken to change direction without the slightest forewarning.

The reader who is unaware of the Qur'ān's uniqueness is often puzzled when he finds it contrary to his understanding of a book in general and a "religious" book in particular. Hence, the Qur'ān may seem disorganised and haphazard to him. However, to those who understand its subject matter, aim and its central theme, the Qur'ān is exactly the opposite. The subject matter of the Qur'ān is essentially man: man in relation to his Lord and Creator, Allāh; man in relation to himself; and man in relation to the rest of creation. The aim and object of the revelations is to invite man to the right way of dealing with his Lord, with himself, and with creation. Hence, the main theme that runs throughout the Qur'ān is that God alone deserves worship and thus, man should submit to God's laws in his personal life and in his relationships with creation in general. Or, in other words, the main theme is a call to the belief in Allāh and the doing of righteous deeds as defined by Allāh.

If the reader keeps these basic facts in mind, he will find that, from beginning to end, the Qur'ān's topics are all closely connected to its main theme and that the whole book is a well-reasoned and cohesive argument for its theme. The Qur'ān keeps the same object in view, whether it is describing the creation of man and the universe or events from human history. Since the aim of the Qur'ān is to guide man, it states or discusses things only to the extent relevant to this aim and leaves out unnecessary and irrelevant details. It also repeats its main theme over and over again in the presentation of each new topic.

In the preface of one of the best orientalist translations of the Qur'ān, the translator, Arthur John Arberry, writes: "There is a repertory of familiar themes running through the whole Koran; each Sura[6] elaborates or adumbrates[7] one or more—often many—of these. Using the language of music, each Sura is a rhapsody composed of whole or fragmentary *leitmotivs*;[8] the analogy is reinforced by the subtly varied rhythmical flow of the discourse."[9]

The following four principles should be kept in mind by the new reader of the Qur'ān if he or she is to avoid unnecessary confusion and disorientation:

1. The book is the only one of its type in the world.

2. Its literary style is quite different from all other books.

3. Its theme is unique.

4. Preconceived notions of a book are only a hindrance to the understanding of the Qur'ān.[10]

THE MIRACLE OF THE QUR'ĀN

Man has a natural distaste towards submitting to another man unless he is forced to by the latter's physical strength or his mental superiority, or if he is shown feats far beyond the

---

[6] Qur'ānic chapter.

[7] Indicate faintly or in outline.

[8] Recurring features.

[9] *The Koran Interpreted*, p. 28.

[10] *The Meaning of the Qur'an*, vol. 1, p. 7.

abilities of any man. In the first two cases, he yields reluctantly, while in the third, he yields because of his belief in a higher force or power defying all human comparison. Therefore, Allāh favoured His messengers not only with revelation, but also with miracles, clearly proving to the people the divine origin and truthfulness of their messages. The inability of the people to imitate the miracles of the prophets made them willingly bear witness to Allāh's unity and obey the commandments of the prophets.

Due to the difficulties involved in communication and transportation, the early prophets were sent only to the people among whom they were raised up. Thus, the miracles which they brought were particularly suited to the areas of knowledge in which their people excelled in order for the miracles to have maximum effect on them. For example, Prophet Mūsā (Moses), may Allāh's peace be on him, was raised up among the Egyptians, who were noted for their mastery of the occult arts, sorcery, and magic. Hence, Allāh gave Prophet Mūsā the miracle of being able to place his hand in his cloak and extract a brilliantly shining hand. And when sorcerers and magicians were gathered to challenge Prophet Mūsā, and the staffs which they had cast appeared to the audience as snakes, Allāh turned Prophet Mūsā's staff into a huge, real snake that devoured the "snakes" of his opponents. That defeat was sufficient proof for the magicians and sorcerers, who knew that no one could change the nature of a stick as Mūsā apparently had done. They fell on their faces in submission and sincere belief in the God of Mūsā, in spite of the threats on their lives uttered by their master, the Pharaoh.

Another example is that of Prophet 'Īsā (Jesus), who was chosen by Allāh from among the Jews. The Jews were especially noted for their exceptional abilities in the field of medicine. Jewish doctors were highly respected and revered for their seemingly magical ability to mend bones, heal wounds, and cure the sick. Thus, Allāh favoured Prophet 'Īsā with the miraculous ability to make the blind see, the lame walk, and to bring the dead back to life. These abilities were clearly beyond those of the Jewish doctors of that day, and they knew well that no regular man could do them. Yet, Allāh gave Prophet ʿĪsā an even more dazzling miracle: he was able to mould birds out of clay, breathe on them, and they would fly away.

Since the Prophet Muḥammad (ﷺ) was to be the last of the prophets sent not only to a particular people, but to all of mankind, he was given a miracle which not only amazed people among whom he was raised, but which would challenge and amaze the human mind until the last days of this world. Prophet Muḥammad (ﷺ), like the other prophets before him, was given a number of other miracles whose effects were basically limited to the people of his time; for example, the splitting of the moon upon his tribe's request for a sign, the outpouring of water from his hands on one occasion when he and his companions were short of water, and the phenomenon of pebbles and rocks giving salāms to him (i.e., greeting him with the phrase: "*al-salāmu ʿalaykum*," meaning, "peace be on you"), just to mention a few.[11] However, the miracle of Prophet Muḥammad (ﷺ) which was consistent with Allāh's aid to the prophets before him was a literary miracle.

The Arabs had very little in the way of unique skills or accumulated knowledge, but they took great pride in their oratory and literary skills. Yearly contests were held in fairs like that of ʿUkāẓ, in which many lines of speeches and poetry were recited from memory. Their language had reached its peak of development, and eloquence was considered the highest quality a man could possess. In fact, ten of the most famous poems were so revered that they were etched in gold and hung in the Kaʿbah for solemn adoration.[12] Consequently,

[11] See *Sahih al-Bukhari*, vol. 5, p. 336, no. 473; vol. 6, p. 365, no. 387; and *Sahih Muslim*, vol. 4, p. 1230, no. 5654.

[12] See *The Concise Encyclopaedia of Islam*, pp. 277-8.

Allāh revealed to His last prophet a book, beginning some of the parts with unintelligible letters like, "*Alif Lām Mīm*" or "*Qāf*" or "*Nūn*," tantalizing the Arab mind, as if to say, "From these letters which you combine to form your daily conversations, as well as great works of prose and poetry, is formed a book whose shortest chapter does not exceed three lines, yet you cannot imitate it, no matter how hard you try!" Thus, his standing miracle was none other then the Qur'ān itself, as the Prophet (ﷺ) himself stated,

مَا مِنَ الأَنْبِيَاءِ مِنْ نَبِيٍّ إِلاَّ قَدْ أُعْطِيَ مِنَ الآيَاتِ مَا مِثْلُهُ آمَنَ عَلَيْهِ الْبَشَرُ،

وَإِنَّمَا كَانَ الَّذِي أُوتِيتُ وَحْيًا أَوْحَى اللهُ إِلَيَّ، فَأَرْجُو أَنْ أَكُونَ أَكْثَرَهُمْ

تَابِعًا يَوْمَ الْقِيَامَةِ

> *"All prophets were given something which would cause people to believe in them. The thing which I was given is none other than a revelation (the Qur'ān) which Allāh revealed to me. So I hope that I will have the most followers among them on the Day of Judgment."*[13]

The Challenge

The Qur'ān is not only unique in the way in which it presents its subject matter, but it is also unique in that it is a miracle itself. By the term "miracle," we mean the performance of a supernatural or extraordinary event which cannot be duplicated by humans. It has been documented that Prophet Muḥammad (ﷺ) challenged the Arabs to produce a literary

---

[13] Reported by Abū Hurayrah in *Sahih al-Bukhari*, vol. 6, p. 474, no. 504; and *Sahih Muslim*, vol. 1, pp. 90-1, no. 283.

work of a similar calibre as the Qur'ān, but they were unable to do so in spite of their well-known eloquence and literary powers. The challenge to reproduce the Qur'ān was presented to the Arabs and mankind in three stages:

1. The Whole Qur'ān:

In the Qur'ān, Allāh commanded the Prophet (ﷺ) to challenge all of creation to create a book of the stature of the Qur'ān:

قُل لَّئِنِ ٱجْتَمَعَتِ ٱلْإِنسُ وَٱلْجِنُّ عَلَىٰٓ أَن يَأْتُوا۟ بِمِثْلِ هَـٰذَا
ٱلْقُرْءَانِ لَا يَأْتُونَ بِمِثْلِهِۦ وَلَوْ كَانَ بَعْضُهُمْ لِبَعْضٍ ظَهِيرًا ﴿٨٨﴾

"Say: 'If all mankind and the jinn would come together to produce the like of this Qur'ān, they could not produce its like even though they exerted all their strength in aiding one another.'"

Sūrah al-Isrā' (17):88.

2. Ten *Sūrahs*:

Next, Allāh made the challenge ostensibly easier by asking those who denied its divine origin to imitate even ten *Sūrahs* of the Qur'ān:

أَمْ يَقُولُونَ ٱفْتَرَىٰهُ ۖ قُلْ فَأْتُوا۟ بِعَشْرِ سُوَرٍ مِّثْلِهِۦ مُفْتَرَيَـٰتٍ
وَٱدْعُوا۟ مَنِ ٱسْتَطَعْتُم مِّن دُونِ ٱللَّهِ إِن كُنتُمْ صَـٰدِقِينَ ﴿١٣﴾

"Or do they say that he has invented it? Say (to them), 'Bring ten invented Sūrahs like it, and call (for help) on whomever you can beside Allāh, if you are truthful.'"

Sūrah Hūd (11):13.

The final challenge was to produce even a single *Sūrah* to match what is in the Qur'ān, whose shortest *Sūrah*, *al-Kawthar*, consists of only three verses:

وَإِن كُنتُمْ فِي رَيْبٍ مِّمَّا نَزَّلْنَا عَلَىٰ عَبْدِنَا فَأْتُوا بِسُورَةٍ مِّن
مِّثْلِهِ وَادْعُوا شُهَدَاءَكُم مِّن دُونِ اللَّهِ إِن كُنتُمْ صَادِقِينَ

"And if you all are in doubt about what We have revealed to Our servant, bring a single Sūrah like it, and call your witnesses besides Allāh if you are truthful."
Sūrah al-Baqarah, (the 87th *Sūrah* revealed) (2):23

These challenges were not just empty words with no one caring to prove them wrong. Prophet Muḥammad's (ﷺ) call to monotheism, to the abolition of idolatry in all its forms, and to the equality of slaves and their masters threatened the whole socio-economic framework of Makkan society in general, and the position of the ruling Qurayshī tribe from which the Prophet (ﷺ) came in particular. Makkah, the trading centre of Arabia, as well as its spiritual centre, desperately wanted to stop the spread of Islām. Yet all that the Prophet's opponents had to do to crush the movement was to make up a single *Sūrah* like any one of those which the Prophet (ﷺ) and his followers were reciting to the people. A number of Qurayshī orators and poets tried to imitate the Qur'ān, but they failed. They then resorted to offering him vast amounts of wealth, the position of king over them, and the most noble and beautiful of their women in exchange for his promise to stop inviting people to Islām. He responded to them by reciting the first thirteen verses of *Sūrah Fuṣṣilat*, until they asked him to stop.[14] The Quraysh also resorted to torturing their slaves and relatives who had embraced Islām in a vain attempt to

[14] Collected by al-Ḥākim, al-Bayhaqī, Abū Ya'lā and Ibn Hishām, and authenticated in *Ṣaḥīḥ al-Sīrah al-Nabawiyyah*, p.64.

cause them to revert to paganism. Later, they organised an economic boycott against the Prophet (ﷺ), his followers and the members of his clan, Banu Hāshim, in an attempt to starve them into submission. But even this plan eventually failed. Finally, they plotted to kill him in his home by sending armed young men from each of the clans of Quraysh in order that the guilt of his murder be shared by all the clans, making revenge by the Prophet's clan impossible.

However, Allāh enabled the Prophet (ﷺ) and his followers to flee Makkah and join a new band of converts who had arisen among the tribes of a city to the north called Yathrib. Islām spread rapidly through the clans of Yathrib, and within a year Muslims became the city's majority. Prophet Muḥammad (ﷺ) was then made the ruler, and the name of the city was changed to Madīnah. Over the next eight years, the clans of Makkah and its neighbouring lands mounted a series of unsuccessful battle campaigns against the emerging Muslim state in Madīnah, which ended with the Muslim invasion of Makkah itself.

All of this bloodshed could have been avoided if only the Quraysh and their allies had been able to produce a mere three lines of poetry or flowing prose similar to the shortest *Sūrah* of the Qur'ān. Hence, there can be no doubt about the inimitability of the Qur'ān's literary style, about the miracle of its rhyme and the marvel of its rhythm.

It has been suggested that the inimitability of the Qur'ān is not necessarily unique, for great English poets like Shakespeare, Chaucer, or great poets in any language tend to have distinctly unique styles which set them apart from their contemporaries. However, if, for example, some leading poet of today was to make an in-depth study of Shakespeare's writings and write a sonnet in Shakespeare's style in old ink and on old paper, then claim that he had discovered a lost poem of Shakespeare's; the literary world would probably accept this claim, even after careful study. Thus, even the greatest of poets could be imitated, no matter how unique his style was, just as famous painters have been imitated.[15] The Qur'ān, however, is way above this level, as attempts to forge chapters have been made throughout the ages, yet none has withstood close scrutiny. And, as was mentioned before, the incentive to imitate the Qur'ān was more intense during the time of its revelation when literary skills were at their peak than at any other time, yet there was no successful attempt.

Other Aspects of the Qur'ān's Miraculous Nature

For a scripture to qualify as divinely revealed, it must be totally accurate in its descriptions of reality: the past, the present and the future. The Qur'ān has many stories about previous prophets and their peoples. Some of these stories have elements in them that can be checked out for their accuracy.

One example of the Qur'ān's precision in its historical descriptions is in the story of Prophet Yūsuf, who was sold as a slave in Egypt, but rose to become an important official in the government, which made it possible for him to bring his whole family to live there in honour. Most historians agree that the entry of the Children of Israel into Egypt occurred when the northern half of the country was ruled by the Hyksos, Semitic invaders who were the first non-Egyptians to rule that country since the rise of the Old Kingdom. The Qur'ān always calls the Egyptian ruler who confronted Moses by the title of "Pharaoh." Every Egyptian ruler was called by this title starting from the reign of Amenhotep IV in the 14th century BC, but not before that. Yūsuf lived at least two hundred years before Amenhotep IV. The Qur'ān consistently refers to the ruler in Yūsuf's time, as "*al-malik*," the king:

---

[15] In fact, some English scholars consider much of what has been attributed to Shakespeare to have been written by his contemporary, Christopher Marlowe.

وَقَالَ ٱلْمَلِكُ ٱئْتُونِى بِهِۦ ۖ

"The king said, 'Bring him to me.'"
Sūrah Yūsuf (12):50.

It should be noted that the Bible refers to the ruler of Joseph's time as "Pharaoh," which was an anachronism inserted by the scribes who wrote the books of the Old Testament centuries after Moses.[16]

Some critics have seized on certain details to try to attack the Qur'ān's historical accuracy. A famous example is the statement of the people to Mary (Ar. Maryam) when she appeared with the baby Jesus after giving birth to him in an isolated place:

يَٰٓأُخْتَ هَٰرُونَ مَا كَانَ أَبُوكِ ٱمْرَأَ سَوْءٍ وَمَا كَانَتْ
أُمُّكِ بَغِيًّا ﴿٢٨﴾

"O sister of Aaron! Your father was not an evil man nor was your mother a prostitute!"
Sūrah Maryam (19):28.

The critics argue that the author confused two historical figures: Mary, the mother of Jesus, and Miriam, the sister of Aaron. The confusion here is really a result of their ignorance about how the Arabs use their language. The Qur'ān refers to Prophet Hūd as the brother of 'Ād:

وَٱذْكُرْ أَخَا عَادٍ إِذْ أَنذَرَ قَوْمَهُۥ بِٱلْأَحْقَافِ

"And mention the brother of 'Ād when he warned his people among the sand dunes."
Sūrah al-Aḥqāf (46):21.

---

[16] *Moses and Pharaoah: The Hebrews in Egypt*, p.176.

The Arabs refer to tribes by the patriarch from whom they are descended. The tribe of ʿĀd was descended from a man named ʿĀd. Hūd was not literally that man's brother, nor was he literally the brother of every member of his tribe, but this was an expression used by the Arabs to indicate association with a people. Mary was a descendant of Aaron. That is why she is referred to as the sister of Aaron. In a similar usage, the New Testament refers to Elizabeth, the mother of John the Baptist as a daughter of Aaron.[17]

Predictions about the Future

The Qur'ān accurately predicted the military victory of the Romans (Byzantines) over the Persians:

غُلِبَتِ ٱلرُّومُ ﴿٢﴾ فِىٓ أَدْنَى ٱلْأَرْضِ وَهُم مِّنۢ بَعْدِ
غَلَبِهِمْ سَيَغْلِبُونَ ﴿٣﴾ فِى بِضْعِ سِنِينَ

"The Romans have been defeated in the nearest land; and after their defeat they will conquer, within a few years."
Sūrah al-Rūm (30):2-4

The Arabic word *biḍʿ* is more precise than the English word "few." Biḍʿ is used for a number between three and ten. The Persians dealt the Romans a crushing defeat in the year 616 CE, taking away Greater Syria and Egypt from them and eventually besieging them in their capital of Constantinople. In 622 CE, the Byzantines won a decisive victory against the Persians at the battle of Issus, which allowed them to regain all the lands they had lost.[18]

---

[17] Luke 1:5.

[18] See *The Holy Qur-an: English Translation of the Meanings and Commentary*, pp. 1202-1203.

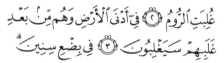

The Qur'ān also accurately predicted that the Muslims would be able to enter Makkah peacefully in order to make *ʿumrah*, the Lesser Pilgrimage.[19] The prediction came in the middle of a long bitter war between the Muslims and the idol worshippers who ruled Makkah. It also promised the Muslims that if they fulfilled the conditions of complete faith and good deeds that Allāh would deputize them to rule the world and would establish their religion and replace the fear they were currently living in with security.[20] That is precisely what happened.

Descriptions of Natural Phenomenon

The Qur'ān calls the reader's attention to numerous natural phenomena that are indicators of Allāh's power, wisdom mercy, etc. As humanity's understanding of the workings of the natural has increased, the miraculous nature of these Qur'ānic descriptions has become manifest. This is not the forum for a detailed discussion of this issue, but a few examples are mentioned by way of illustration:

وَٱلسَّمَآءَ بَنَيۡنَٰهَا بِأَيۡيْدٖ وَإِنَّا لَمُوسِعُونَ ﴿٤٧﴾

"The heaven I created by might, and, verily, I am expanding it."
Sūrah al-Dhāriyāt (51):47.

The Arabic word *mūsʿiūn* is an active participle. It indicates an ongoing action that is occurring at the present time and will continue into the future. It was not until the invention of the spectrograph and the development of a huge (100 in. diameter) reflecting telescope that Edward Hubble was able to discover other galaxies in 1926 and to document in 1927 the red shift of their spectra that indicates they are moving

[19] *Sūrah al-Fatḥ* (48):27.

[20] *Sūrah al-Nūr* (24):55.

away from ours. The Encyclopaedia Britannica says about this: "The implications of this discovery were immense. The universe, *long considered static, was expanding.*"[21]

Allāh says in *Sūrah al-Nūr*:

أَلَمْ تَرَ أَنَّ ٱللَّهَ يُزْجِى
سَحَابًا ثُمَّ يُؤَلِّفُ بَيْنَهُۥ ثُمَّ يَجْعَلُهُۥ رُكَامًا فَتَرَى ٱلْوَدْقَ يَخْرُجُ مِنْ
خِلَٰلِهِۦ وَيُنَزِّلُ مِنَ ٱلسَّمَآءِ مِن جِبَالٍ فِيهَا مِنۢ بَرَدٍ فَيُصِيبُ بِهِۦ مَن يَشَآءُ
وَيَصْرِفُهُۥ عَن مَّن يَشَآءُ

"Have you not seen how Allāh makes the clouds move gently, then joins them together, then makes them a heap? And you see raindrops issuing from their midst. He sends down hail from the sky from mountains of hail therein, causing it to fall on whom he wills and averting it from whom he wills."
Sūrah al-Nūr (24):43.

Gulf News of Friday, May 30th, 1997 carried the following item:

> Earth is bathed by a steady "cosmic rain" of previously undetected objects from outer space that pour vast quantities of water into the atmosphere, according to startling new evidence released Wednesday.
>
> The objects, 20 to 40-ton snowballs the size of two-bedroom houses, streak into the atmosphere by the thousands each day, disintegrate harmlessly 600 to

[21] *The New Encyclopaedia Britannica*, vol. 6, p. 114.

> 15,000 miles up and deposit large clouds of water vapour that eventually falls on Earth's surface as rain, according to Louis A. Frank of the University of Iowa. He led the research team that for the first time has captured images of these objects...taken at both ultraviolet and visible wavelengths by Frank's specially designed instrument aboard NASA's year old Polar spacecraft.[22]

These examples are just the "tip of the iceberg." There are other remarkably accurate statements about oceanography, geology, cosmogony, physics, biology, embryology, etymology, hydrology and other subjects.[23]

Contradictions in the Qur'ān

The Qur'ān challenges its readers to find any errors in it if they do not believe it is really from God:

أَفَلَا يَتَدَبَّرُونَ ٱلْقُرْءَانَ ۚ وَلَوْ كَانَ مِنْ عِندِ غَيْرِ ٱللَّهِ لَوَجَدُوا۟
فِيهِ ٱخْتِلَٰفًا كَثِيرًا ﴿٨٢﴾

"Will they not consider the Qur'ān carefully? Had it been from other than Allāh, they would have found many contradictions in it."
Sūrah al-Nisā' (4):82.

The few apparent "contradictions" commonly mentioned by critics are easily explained.

---

[22] *Gulf News*, Friday, May 30th, 1997, p. 10.

[23] For further reading, see *The Qur'an and Modern Science*, by Maurice Bucaille and *The Amazing Qur'an*, by Gary Miller.

Case One:

One critic writes: "Calling together or ripping apart? In the process of creation, heaven and earth were first apart and are called to come together [41:11], while 21:31 states they were originally one piece and then ripped apart."

First, let us look at the text of each verse. Verse 30 of *Sūrah al-Anbiyā'* states:

أَوَلَمْ يَرَ ٱلَّذِينَ كَفَرُوٓا۟
أَنَّ ٱلسَّمَٰوَٰتِ وَٱلْأَرْضَ كَانَتَا رَتْقًا فَفَتَقْنَٰهُمَا

"Have not those who disbelieved known that the heavens and the earth were joined together, then I[24] *split them apart?"*

On the other hand, verses 11 and 12 of *Sūrah Fuṣṣilat* say:

ثُمَّ ٱسْتَوَىٰٓ إِلَى ٱلسَّمَآءِ وَهِىَ دُخَانٌ
فَقَالَ لَهَا وَلِلْأَرْضِ ٱئْتِيَا طَوْعًا أَوْ كَرْهًا قَالَتَآ أَتَيْنَا طَآئِعِينَ ﴿١١﴾
فَقَضَىٰهُنَّ سَبْعَ سَمَٰوَاتٍ فِى يَوْمَيْنِ وَأَوْحَىٰ فِى كُلِّ سَمَآءٍ أَمْرَهَا

"And[25] *He (it is who) turned to the heaven, when it was smoke and said to it and the earth: 'Come, both of you willingly or unwillingly!'—to which both responded, 'We come in obedience.' And He decreed that they become seven heavens in two periods of time, and imparted unto each heaven its function."*

---

[24] 'We' in the original Arabic, known as the 'majestic or royal we,' is used in reference to Allāh and means 'I'.

[25] The Arabic word is *thumma*. It is a conjunction which sometimes indicates an order of events and sometimes doesn't. Muḥammad Asad understood it not to be ordinal here, so he translated it as 'and.'

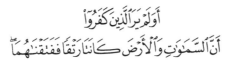

It is surprising that a critic educated in an American university would find a contradiction between these two verses, considering that the dominant theory of cosmogony taught in such universities is the Big Bang theory. According to astronomers and physicists, all the matter in the universe emerged from a state of extremely high density and temperature, which then split apart in an explosion that lead to a rapid decrease in temperature and density. This allowed for the formation of certain atomic nuclei. They say that after a million years, the universe was sufficiently cool for hydrogen and helium atoms to form. After a few hundred million years, fluctuations in density in the expanding gas cloud led to an eventual separation into galaxies, from which individual stars coalesced.[26] This model envisions two stages in the process of creation. The first is an unimaginably dense solid mass. The second is an expanding cloud of high energy particles which eventually cooled enough to be called a gas cloud, from which the galaxies formed.

The two Qur'ānic passages cited by this critic describe two stages in the history of the universe. Neither passage explicitly indicates which state came first, but it is not far-fetched to suppose that there was an original compacted mass that was split asunder, which led to a gaseous ("smoke") stage, from which the heavens then became differentiated.

Case Two:

The same critic writes: "What was man created from? A blood clot [96:1-2], water [21:30, 24:45, 25:54], 'sounding' (i.e. burned) clay [15:26], dust [3:59, 30:20, 35:11], nothing [19:67] and this is then denied in 52:35, earth [11:61], or a drop of thickened fluid [16:4, 75:37]."

Let us look at the verses cited:

---

[26] See *The New Encylopaedia Britannica*, vol. 16, pp. 776-7.

أَوَلَا يَذْكُرُ ٱلْإِنسَٰنُ أَنَّا خَلَقْنَٰهُ مِن قَبْلُ وَلَمْ يَكُ شَيْـًٔا ﴿٦٧﴾

"Doesn't the human being remember that I created him before, when he was nothing."
Sūrah Maryam (19):67.

أَمْ خُلِقُوا۟ مِنْ غَيْرِ شَىْءٍ أَمْ هُمُ ٱلْخَٰلِقُونَ ﴿٣٥﴾

"Were they created from nothing or were they themselves the creators?"
Sūrah al-Ṭūr (52):35.

وَجَعَلْنَا مِنَ ٱلْمَآءِ كُلَّ شَىْءٍ حَىٍّ ۖ

"And I created every living thing from water."
Sūrah al-Anbiyā' (21):30.

وَٱللَّهُ خَلَقَ كُلَّ دَآبَّةٍ مِّن مَّآءٍ ۖ

"And Allāh created every crawling creature from water."
Sūrah al-Nūr (24):45.

وَهُوَ ٱلَّذِى خَلَقَ مِنَ ٱلْمَآءِ بَشَرًا

"And He it is who created man from water."
Sūrah al-Furqān (25):54.

وَلَقَدْ خَلَقْنَا ٱلْإِنسَٰنَ مِن صَلْصَٰلٍ مِّنْ حَمَإٍ مَّسْنُونٍ ﴿٢٦﴾

"And, indeed, I have created man out of sounding clay, out of dark, smooth mud transmuted."[27]
Sūrah al-Ḥijr (15):26.

هُوَ أَنشَأَكُم مِّنَ ٱلْأَرْضِ

"He (Allāh) brought you forth from the earth."
Sūrah Hūd (11):62.

وَمِنْ ءَايَٰتِهِۦٓ أَنْ خَلَقَكُم مِّن تُرَابٍ

"And among His signs is that He created you from dust."
Sūrah Rūm (30):20.

ٱقْرَأْ بِٱسْمِ رَبِّكَ ٱلَّذِى خَلَقَ ﴿١﴾ خَلَقَ ٱلْإِنسَٰنَ مِنْ عَلَقٍ ﴿٢﴾

"Read in the name of your Lord who has created — created man from a clinging thing."[28]
Sūrah al-'Alaq (96:1-2).

أَلَمْ يَكُ نُطْفَةً مِّن مَّنِىٍّ يُمْنَىٰ ﴿٣٧﴾

"Was he not a drop of fluid that gushed forth?"
Sūrah al-Qiyāmah (75):37.

خَلَقَ ٱلْإِنسَٰنَ مِن نُّطْفَةٍ فَإِذَا هُوَ خَصِيمٌ مُّبِينٌ ﴿٤﴾

"He created the human being from a drop of fluid, then, behold, he becomes an open opponent."
Sūrah al-Naḥl (16):4.

---

[27] The term '*ṣalṣāl*' used in this verse means 'clay mixed with sand, which, when dried makes a sound' (i.e., when it is struck.). *Arabic-English Lexicon*, vol. 2 , p. 1711.

[28] The word "*alaq*' is more accurately translated as 'a clinging thing' rather than 'a blood clot' in this context.

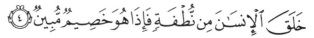

The perception of contradiction here is a result of confusion between metaphysics, chemistry and biology, and between different stages of the process of biological creation. The first two verses above are dealing with creation in metaphysical terms. In the first verse, Allāh reminds human beings that He created them and all of creation ultimately from nothing, which is one of His most sublime attributes. In the second verse, He poses a rhetorical question to highlight the untenable implication of atheism, "If you deny the existence of God, then do you believe that nothingness brought you into existence?" Therefore, there is no contradiction between these two verses.

The next three verses state that all living creatures, including those that crawl and human beings, are created from water. This is a biological fact that no one denies. All living creatures have water-based physiologies.

The next set of verses state that the human being was created from dust and clay and was brought forth from the earth. There are two acceptable *tafsīrs* for these verses. One is that they refer to Adam, the ancestor of mankind. The other is that they refer to the chemical composition of every human being. The elements of carbon, hydrogen, nitrogen, etc. are present in the earth. Through photosynthesis, these elements are transformed into vegetable matter, which human beings consume directly or by eating the flesh of animals that have consumed plants. The source of all living creatures is thus, ultimately, the earth, or, by another expression, the dust of the earth, which when combined with water is called 'clay.'

The rest of the verses refer to the biological aspects of human creation. The word *nuṭfah* is commonly used to refer to male seminal fluid, but it is also linguistically possible to use it to refer to the female reproductive fluids. The fertilized zygote is referred to in the Qur'ān as *nuṭfah amshāj*, that is, 'a mingled fluid'.[29] In a *ḥadīth*, the word *nuṭfah* is explicitly used to refer to the fluid of the woman. It was reported that the Prophet (ﷺ) was asked from what the human being was created, to which he replied,

مِنْ كُلٍّ يُخْلَقُ ، مِنْ نُطْفَةِ الرَّجُلِ ، وَمِنْ نُطْفَةِ الْمَرْأَةِ

"He is created from both the nuṭfah of the man and the nuṭfah of the woman."[30]

After fertilization, the embryo implants itself in the uterine wall. It is at this stage that it is called an *ʿalaq* in Arabic.[31] Therefore, there is no contradiction between any of these verses, *alḥamdulillāh*.

The Numerical Miracle of the Qur'ān

The most famous proponent of this idea was Rashad Khalifa, an Egyptian biochemist educated in the United States. According to Dr. Khalifa, there is a miraculous numerical code to the Qur'ān based on its "first" verse (*Bismillāhir-Raḥmānir-Raḥīm*), which consists of 19 letters. This miraculous code is supposedly referred to in verse 30 of Chapter 74 (*al-Muddaththir*) which states "Over it are 19." Based on these two premises, Dr. Rashad claims to have

---

[29] *Sūrah al-Insān* (76):2. There is a wonderful subtlety in this expression that puzzled early commentators; the word *nuṭfah* is a singular noun, while the word *amshāj* is a plural adjective, which is not a normal Arabic construction. The *nuṭfah* is a single entity after fertilisation, but its chromosomes are half from the father and half from the mother. "Therefore, from the scientific point of view, *amshāj* is entirely accurate as a plural adjective modifying the singular *nuṭfah*, which is really a multifaceted single entity." *The Qur'an and Modern Science: Correlation Studies*, pp. 27-9.

[30] *Musnad Ahmad*, no. 4206. The *isnād* has weakness in it due to the presence of al-Ḥusayn ibn al-Ḥasan al-Fazārī, who was truthful but prone to mistakes. (See *Taqrīb al-Tahdhīb*, p. 166, no. 1317.) This part of the *ḥadīth* is supported by the *ḥadīth* of ʿAbdullāh ibn Salām reported by al-Bukhārī which mentions that if the fluid of the woman (*mā' al-mar'ah*) supersedes the fluid of the man, then the child will resemble the mother. (*Sahih al-Bukhari*, vol. 5, pp. 189-90, no. 275.)

[31] *The Qur'an and Modern Science: Correlation Studies*, p.31.

discovered an intricate mathematical pattern involving 19 and its multiples throughout the Qur'ān and especially in what he calls the Qur'ānic initials which precede 29 chapters (*Alif*, *Lām*, *Mīm*, etc.). From this discovery, Dr. Khalifa concludes that the complexity of this mathematical code's pattern in a literary work of the Qur'ān's size is far beyond human capabilities, and that it alone constitutes the only real miracle of the Qur'ān which proves its divine origin.[32] He further concludes that 19 and its multiples represent the key to the correct interpretation of the Qur'ān and Islām, and the reason why 19 was chosen is because it means "God is One," which is the message of the Qur'ān.[33]

Many Muslims at first received Khalifa's theories with uncritical enthusiasm. However, when more rigorous critics began checking his numbers, they found numerous discrepancies and some outright fabrications in his data. His claims were based on the number of times a given letter or word occurs in a given *Sūrah* or group of *Sūrahs*. It was discovered that he would sometimes treat *hamzahs* like *alifs* and sometimes he wouldn't, depending on the totals he needed in a given *Sūrah* to confirm his theory. Sometimes he counted letters that weren't there, sometimes he failed to count existing letters, sometimes he counted two words as one, sometimes he added to the Qur'ānic text and sometimes he deleted from it, all for the purpose of making the letter and word counts conform to his theory. On top of that, his letter counts changed over time, depending on whether he wanted to establish a pattern for a *Sūrah* by itself or as part of a group of *Sūrahs*. When confronted with inconsistencies in his data, he began claiming that certain verses had been inserted into the Qur'ān that did

---

[32] See Rashad Khalifa's presentation of his theory in the article "*Problem of 19*," *Impact International*, 13-26 Nov., 1981, pp.14-15.

[33] *Quran: Visual Presentation of The Miracle*, pp.70-73, 243. Note: This calculation is based on the *Abjad* system of numerology in which the letters of the Arabic alphabet are given numerical values, a system borrowed from the Jewish mystical system known as *Kabbalah*.

not belong there. After this clear statement of disbelief, he went on to claim knowledge of the exact date of the Day of Judgment and eventually claimed prophethood for himself. He attracted a group of followers in Tucson, Arizona, but his career was cut short when he was stabbed to death by an unknown assailant in 1990.[34]

---

[34] See *Mission to America*, pp. 137-168. A detailed refutation of this theory can be found in my book, *The Quran's Numerical Miracle: Hoax and Heresy*.

TAFSĪR SŪRAH AL-MULK

67

Name of the *Sūrah*

The word *mulk* is derived from the verb *malaka*, which means "to possess or own exclusively". Consequently, the noun *mulk* means "dominion", "sovereignty", "kingship", "owner-ship", "possession" and "authority."[35]

The name *mulk* is taken from the first verse of the chapter. However, it should be noted that most of the names of the chapters were not mentioned by the Prophet (ﷺ) himself and, as such, we can find in some recent copies of the Qur'ān that the ninth *Sūrah* is entitled *al-Tawbah* while, in others it is entitled *al-Barā'ah*. In fact, statements of the Prophet (ﷺ) and his companions regarding this chapter indicate that in earlier times it was more commonly titled *Sūrah al-Māniʿah*

[35] *Arabic-English Lexicon*, vol. 2, p. 3023.

or *Tabārak*. This variation in the names does not in any way represent contradictions or changes within the Qur'ān because the majority of chapter titles were chosen by the companions of the Prophet (ﷺ) and scholars of later generations for identification purposes.

There are, however, a few chapters which the Prophet (ﷺ) referred to by titles. For example, the first chapter commonly known as *Sūrah al-Fātiḥah* was referred to by the Prophet (ﷺ) as "*Fātiḥatul-Kitāb*," "*Ummul-Kitāb*," "*Sūratul-Ḥamd*," as well as a variety of other names. These names or titles were used to identify the chapters or to bring out one or more of its important themes. They were not revealed with the Qur'ān and, as such, cannot be considered part of the Qur'ān. Thus, their variations in no way affect the purity and authenticity of the Qur'ān's text.[36]

Place of Revelation

There are no authentic *ḥadīths* to indicate when this chapter was revealed. However, most scholars of *tafsīr* (Qur'ānic exegesis) have concluded from its subject matter and style that it was among the early chapters revealed in Makkah.[37]

The Qur'ān is traditionally divided into thirty portions (*juz'*) in order to facilitate a monthly reading of the whole text, as was recommended by Prophet Muḥammad (ﷺ).[38] This chapter begins the twenty-ninth portion, which is commonly known as *Juz' Tabārak*.

---

[36] See *Tafseer Soorah al-Hujuraat*, pp. 39-40 for a discussion of additions to the Qur'ānic text.

[37] *Al-Mu'jam al-Mufahras li Alfāẓ al-Qur'ān*, p. 754.

[38] "*Read the Qur'ān in one month.*" *Sahih al-Bukhari*, vol. 6, pp. 516-7, no. 572.

The Virtues of the *Sūrah*

This *sūrah* is among the most frequently read chapters of the Qur'ān, based on the special recommendations made by Prophet Muḥammad (ﷺ) about it. Some of these recommendations are accurate, while others have been falsely attributed to the Prophet (ﷺ).[39] The following *ḥadīths* are the authentic narrations regarding *Sūrah al-Mulk*.

Punishment of the Grave

After people die, they enter the world of the *Barzakh*, where they remain until the Day of Resurrection. In that dimension, the fulfilment of divine promise of reward and punishment for the deeds of this life will begin. The Prophet (ﷺ) was recorded as saying that the grave would either be a garden from Paradise or a hole from Hell.[40] 'Abdullāh ibn Mas'ūd related that the Prophet (ﷺ) said,

سُورَةُ تَبَارَكَ هِيَ الْمَانِعَةُ مِنْ عَذَابِ الْقَبْرِ

> *"Sūrah Tabārak is a shield from the punishment of the grave."*[41]

Based on this authentic prophetic tradition, it can be stated with certainty that this chapter will provide protection from the punishment of the grave. The question which arises is how will it be a shield, and for whom will this protection be. The physical and material existence of the chapter are not intended here, because the Prophet (ﷺ) and his companions never used the chapter in this way. Thus, if a copy of the

---

[39] For a list of some of the most common inauthentic *ḥadīths* regarding *Sūrah al-Mulk*, see the appendix at the end of this book.

[40] *Ḍa'īf Sunan al-Tirmidhī*, no. 437.

[41] Collected by al-Dāraquṭnī in *al-'Ilal* (p. 53, no. 5) and authenticated in *Silsilah al-Aḥādīth al-Ṣaḥīḥah*, p. 131, no. 3.

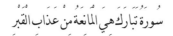

chapter is wrapped in the *kafn* (shroud) of the deceased, it will not be of any benefit. The chapter must be read regularly with understanding in order for it to be a shield. Ibn Mas'ūd was quoted as saying, "Allāh will protect anyone who recites *Tabārakal-ladhī biyadihil-mulk* every night from the punishment of the grave. During the era of the Messenger of Allāh, we used to call it 'the protector'."[42]

The punishment of the grave is for those with a preponderance of evil deeds and is something which every true believer should fear. The Companions, the best generation to have ever lived, did not feel safe from it. Hānī, the freed slave of 'Uthmān, said, "When 'Uthmān ibn 'Affān stood at a grave he would weep until his beard was wet. So it was said to him, 'Indeed you mention Paradise and Hell and you do not weep. Yet you are weeping at this?' He replied, 'Certainly, Allāh's Messenger (ﷺ) said,

إِنَّ الْقَبْرَ أَوَّلُ مَنْزِلٍ مِنْ مَنَازِلِ الْآخِرَةِ فَإِنْ نَجَا مِنْهُ فَمَا بَعْدَهُ أَيْسَرُ مِنْهُ، وَإِنْ لَمْ يَنْجُ مِنْهُ فَمَا بَعْدَهُ أَشَدُّ مِنْهُ . قَالَ : وَقَالَ رَسُولُ اللهِ : مَا رَأَيْتُ مَنْظَرًا قَطُّ إِلَّا

وَالْقَبْرُ أَفْظَعُ مِنْهُ

'Truly the grave is the first abode of the Hereafter. If one is saved from it (i.e. its punishment), then what follows is made easier for him. And if one is not saved from it, then what follows is more severe.' He (ﷺ) also said, 'I have never seen a sight more horrid than the grave.'"[43]

---

[42] *'Amal al-yawm wal-laylah*, pp. 433-4.

[43] *Sunan Ibn Mājah*, vol. 5, pp. 499-500, no. 4267; authenticated in *Ṣaḥīḥ Sunan Ibn Mājah*, vol. 2, p. 421, no. 3442. The *ḥadīth* was also collected by al-Tirmidhī.

Hence, Muslims should be highly motivated to read this *Sūrah*, with the hope of being spared the horrifying punishments of the grave. By reading this chapter and reflecting on its meanings in such a way that it improves the reader's character and increases the reader's righteous deeds, the chapter becomes a shield from the torment of the grave. This method is in keeping with Allāh's instruction:

أَفَلَا يَتَدَبَّرُونَ ٱلْقُرْءَانَ أَمْ عَلَىٰ قُلُوبٍ أَقْفَالُهَآ ﴿٢٤﴾

"Will they not reflect on the Qur'ān, or are their hearts locked up?"
Sūrah Muḥammad (47):24[44]

Consequently, the chapter will be a shield only for the righteous whose good deeds are increased by its regular recitation.

Intercession

In addition, the Prophet (ﷺ) also informed his followers that *Sūrah al-Mulk* will be a source of intercession for some of its readers on the Day of Judgment. Abū Hurayrah related that the Prophet (ﷺ) said,

إِنَّ سُورَةً مِنَ القُرْآنِ ثَلاثُونَ آيَةً شَفَعَتْ لِرَجُلٍ حَتَّى غُفِرَ لَهُ، وَهِيَ سُورَةُ

تَبَارَكَ الَّذِي بِيَدِهِ الْمُلْكُ

"There is a chapter in the Qur'ān containing thirty verses which will continue to intercede for a person until all of his [or her] sins are forgiven. It is Tabārakal-ladhī biyadihil-mulk."[45]

---

[44] See also 4:82

[45] That is, *Sūrah al-Mulk* (67). The *ḥadīth* was collected by al-Tirmidhī, Abū Dāwūd, al-Nasā'ī and Ibn Mājah. The English text can be found in *Sunan Abu Dawud*, vol. 1, p. 367, no. 1395, and it is authenticated in *Ṣaḥīḥ Sunan al-Tirmidhī*, vol. 3, p. 6, no. 2315 and *Ṣaḥīḥ Sunan Abū Dāwūd*, vol. 1, p. 263, no. 1247.

This narration does not specify the categories of people for whom the chapter will intercede. Consequently, it must be understood within the general context of intercession in Islām. The key principle regarding intercession is found in the following Qur'ānic verses:

مَن ذَا ٱلَّذِى يَشْفَعُ عِندَهُۥٓ إِلَّا بِإِذْنِهِۦ ۚ

"Who can intercede with Him except with His permission?"
Sūrah al-Baqarah (2):255.

يَوْمَئِذٍ لَّا تَنفَعُ ٱلشَّفَٰعَةُ إِلَّا مَنْ أَذِنَ لَهُ ٱلرَّحْمَٰنُ وَرَضِىَ لَهُۥ
قَوْلًا ﴿١٠٩﴾

"On that day, no intercession will be of use, except from those whom Allāh permits [to intercede], and whose word is acceptable to Him."
Sūrah Ṭā Hā (20):109.

Intercession is only by the will of Allāh. On the Day of Judgment, Allāh will honour some of His creation, like the angels, the prophets, and certain righteous individuals,[46] by giving them permission to intercede on behalf of some people whom Allāh had already decided would go to Paradise. The Prophet (ﷺ) said,

[46] *Sahih al-Bukhari*, vol. 9, pp. 395-9, no. 532; *Sahih Muslim*, vol. 1, pp. 117-9, no. 352. Included among the righteous are those who died as martyrs. According to the Prophet (ﷺ), they will be permitted to intercede for seventy people of their households. *Sunan Abu Dawud*, vol. 2, p. 699, no. 2516; *Sunan Ibn Majah*, vol. 4, p. 164, no. 2799; authenticated in *Ṣaḥīḥ Sunan Abū Dāwūd*, vol. 2, p. 479, no. 2201. [Also collected by al-Tirmidhī and Aḥmad].

مَنْ قَرَأَ الْقُرْآنَ وَاسْتَظْهَرَهُ فَأَحَلَّ حَلَالَهُ، وَحَرَّمَ حَرَامَهُ أَدْخَلَهُ اللهُ بِهِ الْجَنَّةَ

وَشَفَّعَهُ فِي عَشَرَةٍ مِنْ أَهْلِ بَيْتِهِ كُلُّهُمْ قَدْ وَجَبَتْ لَهُ النَّارُ

"Whoever reads the Qur'ān and implements it, such that he regarded its lawful as lawful and its prohibited as prohibited, Allāh will put him in Paradise, and grant him intercession for ten members of his household, all of whom are deserving of the Fire."[47]

However, intercession will not be an arbitrary right, whereby intercessors will be able to intercede for whomsoever they wish. The fact that intercession is not the prerogative of the intercessor is clearly demonstrated in a narration related by Anas ibn Mālik, in which he quoted the Prophet (ﷺ) as saying,

لَيَرِدَنَّ عَلَيَّ نَاسٌ مِنْ أَصْحَابِي الْحَوْضَ حَتَّى إِذَا عَرَفْتُهُمْ اخْتُلِجُوا دُونِي

فَأَقُولُ: أُصَيْحَابِي، فَيَقُولُ: لَا تَدْرِي مَا أَحْدَثُوا بَعْدَكَ

"Some of my Companions will come to me at my pond [on the Day of Judgment] and after I recognise them, they will be taken away and I will say, 'They are my Companions!' Then it will be said, 'You do not know the innovations they made in the religion after your time."[48]

In spite of the fact that Prophet Muḥammad (ﷺ) will be given permission to intercede for his followers, he will not be able to intercede for this group of his followers because they made

[47] Collected by al-Tirmidhī and Ibn Mājah. *Ḍa'īf Sunan al-Tirmidhī*, p. 348, no. 553.

[48] *Sahih Al-Bukhari*, vol. 8, p. 381, no. 584; *Sahih Muslim*, vol. 4, p. 1239, no. 5706.

changes in the religion of Islām. Abū Hurayrah reported that the Prophet of Allāh (ﷺ) said,

لكل نبي دعوة مستجابة . فتعجل كل نبي دعوته . وإني اختبأت دعوتي

شفاعة لأمتي يوم القيامة . فهي نائلة ، إن شاء الله ، من مات من أمتي

لا يشرك بالله شيئاً

> *"Every messenger was permitted a prayer which would be answered, but all the prophets were hasty in using this prayer (in this life). However, I have reserved my prayer for the intercession of my followers on the Day of Resurrection, and it will be granted, if Allāh so wills,* ***in the case of everyone among my followers, as long as they die without associating any partners with Allāh.****"*[49]

This is a clear reminder to those people who have the mistaken belief that the Prophet (ﷺ) will intercede for everybody who is Muslim and they will all go to Paradise, no matter what they did in this life. This is a delusion similar to the delusion that Jews and Christians are under. Christians believe that their acceptance of Jesus as their Lord guarantees them Paradise, and that actions are of no consequence. Jews, on the other hand, believe that Paradise is their personal property and no one else has a right to it except for them.

If the Prophet (ﷺ) was permitted to intercede freely, without any restriction or limitation, he certainly would have interceded for his own mother and father. However, Anas reported that a person once asked:

---

[49] *Sahih Muslim*, vol. 1, p. 134, no. 389.

يَا رَسُولَ اللَّهِ أَيْنَ أَبِي؟ قَالَ: فِي النَّارِ. فَلَمَّا قَفَّى دَعَاهُ فَقَالَ: إِنَّ أَبِي وَأَبَاكَ فِي النَّارِ

"O Messenger of Allāh, where is my father?" The Prophet replied: "He is in the Fire." When the man turned away, the Prophet (ﷺ) called out to him and said, "Indeed, my father and your father are in the Fire."[50]

Also, Abū Hurayrah related that Allāh's Messenger (ﷺ) visited the grave of his mother. He wept, and moved others around him to tears, and then said,

اسْتَأْذَنْتُ رَبِّي فِي أَنْ أَسْتَغْفِرَ لَهَا فَلَمْ يُؤْذَنْ لِي وَاسْتَأْذَنْتُهُ فِي أَنْ أَزُورَ قَبْرَهَا فَأُذِنَ لِي. فَزُورُوا الْقُبُورَ. فَإِنَّهَا تُذَكِّرُ الْمَوْتَ

"I sought permission from my Lord to beg forgiveness for her, but it was not granted to me; and I sought permission to visit her grave, and it was granted to me. So visit the graves, for that makes you mindful of death."[51]

This may come as a shock to some people, because there is a house in Makkah identified as that of the Prophet's parents, and people go there to make special acts of worship, believing that the father of the Prophet (ﷺ) is going to Paradise. However, the house is not authentically identified and may be considered as one of the fabled sites, like the 'grave' of Eve in Jeddah. Likewise, if the Prophet (ﷺ) was able to independently intercede and remove anyone from Hell, he would surely have

---

[50] *Sahih Muslim*, vol. 1, p. 136 no. 398.

[51] *Sahih Muslim*, vol. 2, p. 463, no. 2130.

done so for his uncle, Abū Ṭālib, for he had raised him like his own son, protected him, and defended him against the Makkan pagans who opposed his prophethood. However, the intercession which was allowed to him for his uncle was limited to reducing the severity of his punishment in Hell.

Abū Saʿīd al-Khudrī reported: The Prophet's uncle Abū Ṭālib was mentioned in the Messenger of Allāh's presence and he said,

لَعَلَّهُ تَنْفَعُهُ شَفَاعَتِي يَوْمَ الْقِيَامَةِ فَيُجْعَلَ فِي ضَحْضَاحٍ مِنَ النَّارِ يَبْلُغُ كَعْبَيْهِ يَغْلِي مِنْهُ دِمَاغُهُ

"My intercession will benefit him on the Day of Resurrection. He will be placed in the shallowest part of the Fire which would reach up to his ankles, causing his brain to boil."[52]

In spite of that, Nuʿmān ibn Bashīr related that Allāh's Messenger (ﷺ) said,

إِنَّ أَهْوَنَ أَهْلِ النَّارِ عَذَاباً مَنْ لَهُ نَعْلَانِ وَشِرَاكَانِ مِنْ نَارٍ ، يَغْلِي مِنْهُمَا دِمَاغُهُ . كَمَا يَغْلِي الْمِرْجَلُ مَا يَرَى أَنَّ أَحَداً أَشَدُّ مِنْهُ عَذَاباً . وَإِنَّهُ لَأَهْوَنُهُمْ عَذَاباً

"Indeed, the inhabitant of the fire suffering the least would be one who will have two shoes and laces of fire on his feet which will cause his brain to boil the way that a cooking vessel boils. And he will think that he could not see anyone suffering a

---

[52] *Sahih Muslim*, vol. 1, p. 139, no. 411.

more grievous punishment than himself, though his punishment would be the least."[53]

There are levels in the Fire as there are levels in Paradise. But the best that the Prophet (ﷺ) could do for his dearly beloved uncle, Abū Ṭālib, who was closer to him than anyone, was to lessen the intensity of the fire. This clearly indicates that intercession is only according to the will of Allāh. He will designate some of the prophets and the righteous to take those whom He has already decided will go to Paradise out of Hell and into Paradise. Intercession will thus be a means of honouring those whom He chooses to honour over the rest of mankind on that day.

Passport to Paradise

Anas ibn Mālik quoted the Prophet (ﷺ) as saying,

سُورَةٌ مِنَ الْقُرْآنِ مَا هِيَ إِلَّا ثَلَاثُونَ آيَةً خَاصَمَتْ عَنْ صَاحِبِهَا حَتَّى

أَدْخَلَتْهُ الْجَنَّةَ، وَهِيَ سُورَةُ تَبَارَكَ

"There is a chapter in the Qur'ān which is only thirty verses. It will argue on behalf of its companion until it gets him into Paradise. It is Sūrah Tabārak."[54]

Prior to Sleep

Consequently, it was the nightly practice of the Prophet to recite *Sūrah al-Mulk* prior to going to sleep. Jābir narrated

---

[53] *Sahih Muslim*, vol. 1, p. 139, no. 415. In another narration by Ibn 'Abbās, he quoted Allāh's Messenger (ﷺ) as saying, *"Abū Ṭālib will have the least suffering among the inhabitants of the fire. He will be wearing two shoes of fire, which will cause his brain to boil."* (*Sahih Muslim*, vol. 1, p. 139, no. 413.)

[54] Collected by al-Ṭabarānī in *al-Mu'jam al-Ṣaghīr*, vol. 1, p. 296. All the narrators are *thiqāt* except Sulaymān ibn Dāwūd ibn Yaḥyā al-Ṭabīb al-Baṣrī. I couldn't find any mention of him in the books of *Tarjumah*.

that Allāh's Messenger (ﷺ) would not go to sleep until he had recited *Alif Lām Mīm, Tanzīl*[55] and *Tabārakal-ladhī bi yadihil-mulk.*[56]

[55] *Sūrah al-Sajdah* (32).

[56] Collected by al-Tirmidhī (*Mishkāt al Maṣābīḥ*, vol. 1, p. 456) and authenticated in *Ṣaḥīḥ Sunan al-Tirmidhī*, vol. 3, p. 6, no. 2316.

VERSE 01

تَبَٰرَكَ ٱلَّذِى بِيَدِهِ ٱلْمُلْكُ وَهُوَ عَلَىٰ كُلِّ شَىْءٍ قَدِيرٌ ﴿١﴾

Blessed is He in Whose Hand is the dominion,[57] *and He is able to do all things.*

Almighty Allāh begins this chapter by praising Himself as being the source of all goodness and blessing. Self-praise is despised among humans because they have many more defects and deficiencies than points of praise. Prophet Muḥammad (ﷺ) changed the names of his followers which indicated self praise. For example, Ibn ʿAbbās related that one of the Prophet's wives was named Barrah (righteous), and he changed it to Juwayriyah (little girl).[58] Jābir ibn ʿAbdullāh reported that the Prophet (ﷺ) forbade names like Yaʿlā (elevated), Barakah (blessing), Aflaḥ (successful), Yasār (wealth) and

---

[57] Note that *mulk* here has a different shade of meaning from *malakūt* in 36:83. Both words are from the same verb *malaka*, and both are commonly translated by the word "dominion". But *malakūt* actually refers to Lordship over the invisible world, while *Mulk* refers to Lordship over the visible world. (*Arabic-English Lexicon*, vol. 2. p. 3023.) Allāh is Lord of both.

[58] *Sahih Muslim*, vol. 3, pp. 1170-1, no. 5334.

Nāfiʿ (beneficial).[59] The appropriate characteristic for human beings is that of humility. This was stressed by the Prophet (ﷺ) in his statement,

مَنْ يَتَوَاضَعْ لِلّٰهِ، سُبْحَانَهُ، دَرَجَةً، يَرْفَعْهُ اللّٰهُ

"Whoever is humble for the sake of Allāh, will be elevated by Him."[60]

Consequently, the Almighty praises Himself to remind His creatures that all praise belongs to Him alone.

Part of His greatness is that the whole world, visible and invisible, is in His Hand. He created it, and administers it as He pleases. No one has the right to question His judgment or His actions. He is Irresistible, His wisdom is infinite, and His justice is perfect. In the created world, there is often a separation between goodness and power; a reality reflected in the popular quote, "Absolute power corrupts absolutely." However, in the divine nature, there is no separation or antagonism.

Allāh uses the phrase "*His hand*" in describing the completeness of His control over His creation. The use of such terms must be understood according to the general verse in which Allāh said:

لَيْسَ كَمِثْلِهِۦ شَىْءٌ ۖ وَهُوَ ٱلسَّمِيعُ ٱلْبَصِيرُ ﴿١١﴾

"Nothing is similar to Him, and He hears all and sees all."
Sūrah al-Shūrā (42):11

---

[59] Ibid., p. 1170, no. 5333.

[60] Authenticated in *Ṣaḥīḥ al-Jāmiʿ al-Ṣaghīr*, vol. 2, p. 1061, no. 6162, where it was attributed to *Ḥilyah al-Awliyā'*. A similar *ḥadīth* was collected in *Sahih Muslim*, vol. 4, p. 1369, no. 6264.

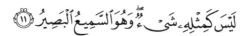

It is grossly incorrect to claim that God has a hand like that of humans, and conceive of Him in human form as many Christians, Hindus and the followers of other religions have done. But, it is also incorrect to deny that Allāh has a hand, since He has attributed to Himself a hand in a number of Qur'ānic verses.[61] The basic rule in understanding such attributes is to accept them as stated, according to their literal meaning, but not to understand them in any way which makes them similar to Allāh's creation. Those who reject the literal meaning of "hand",[62] accept that Allāh has referred to His creatures as "living" (3:27, 21:30) and also referred to Himself as "living" (2:255). They do not negate Allāh's life, simply because to do so would reduce Him to a non-entity. Instead, they rightly stress that the "life" of created beings is much different than the "life" of Allāh. Human and animal life is dependent on Allāh, while Allāh's divine life is independent of His creatures. It is a life without beginning or end. The principle is the same, and should be applied to all of Allāh's attributes similarly. It may be argued that to accept the term "hand" without the concept behind it is impossible. However, the term "hand" is commonly used in English when referring to the hour, minute and second indicators, as the "hands of the clock", without imagining human-like hands.

It should be noted that accepting the "hands of Allāh" literally does not put Muslims in the same position as Christians, who draw, paint and carve pictures of God in human likeness, and use them in worship under the name "icons." Many Judaeo-Christian texts are very explicit in describing God in human

---

[61] 3:73, 5:64, 23:88, 36:83, 38:75, 48:10, 57:29.

[62] For example, Sayyid Abul 'A'la Mawdudi states in *The Meaning of the Quran*, vol. 6, pp. 8-9, "*In Whose hand is the Kingdom* does not mean that He has physical hands, but that He is possessor of all power and authority and no one else has any share in it." However, accepting the literal meaning of "hand" does not necessarily mean that Allāh's hands are like the "physical hands" of His creation. He has a hand befitting His Majesty, the form of which we do not know nor are we supposed to guess.

terms.[63] On the other hand, when Muslim artists in Turkey, Persia and India broke the divine ban on making images of living beings, they painted angels, the Prophet (ﷺ), and other humans and animals, but none ventured to paint a picture of God.

On the basis of God's infinite power, He referred to Himself as being able to do all things. The perfection of His greatness requires that He be capable of doing whatever He wishes. Nothing can frustrate or hinder Him from doing anything He desires. However, it cannot be reasonably argued that since God is able to do all things, He could become a man if He wished, or have a son, if He chose to do so. His ability to do all things does not include the absurd, like those acts which would contradict His divinity. For example, being without beginning and end is part of what makes Him God, so to propose that God could be born or die is ridiculous since it would entail God becoming a being less than God. Likewise, for the Creator to become His creation (i.e., a man or an animal) is for Him to become a creature in need of a Creator. Such absurdities should not be attributed to God. Consequently, it is understood that when God says that He is able to do "all things", it means "all things" befitting His Majesty and consistent with His divinity, and not "things" which would make Him in any way less than God.

---

[63] Genesis 2:2, "And on the seventh day God finished his work which he had done, and he *rested* on the seventh day from all the work which he had done."
Genesis 3:8, "And they heard *the sound of the Lord God walking* in the garden in the cool of the day."
Genesis 32:22, "Jacob *wrestled* God, who said to him, 'Let me go; for the day is breaking."
Genesis 6:6, "And the Lord was *sorry* that he made man on the earth, and it grieved him to his heart."
Exodus 32:14, "And the Lord *repented* of the evil which he thought to do to his people."
Psalm 4:23, "Then the Lord *awaked* as one out of sleep, and a mighty man that shouts by reason of wine."

VERSE 02

ٱلَّذِى خَلَقَ ٱلْمَوْتَ وَٱلْحَيَوٰةَ لِيَبْلُوَكُمْ أَيُّكُمْ أَحْسَنُ عَمَلًا ۚ وَهُوَ ٱلْعَزِيزُ ٱلْغَفُورُ ﴿٢﴾

Who has created death and life, that He may test you, which of you is best in deed. And He is the All-Mighty, the Oft-Forgiving.

In this verse, Allāh continues to describe His infinite powers. He created death. Consequently, death is not merely non-existence. It is an existent creation of Allāh. Prophet Muḥammad (ﷺ) was quoted as saying that on the Day of Judgment, death will appear in the form of a ram which will be slaughtered,[64] signifying the eternal nature of the life to come. Likewise, Allāh created life. His act of creation is unique, in that He created life out of nothing. Human acts of "creation" are really manipulation of what was already created. Death is put before life in this verse as in verse 28 of the chapter *al-Baqarah* (2):

---

[64] The Prophet (ﷺ) was quoted as saying, "*Death will be brought [in the form of] a white ram with black markings and it will be made to stand between heaven and Hell....It will be slaughtered and it will be said, 'Immortality, and no more death.'*" *Sahih Al-Bukhari*, vol. 6, p. 226-7, no. 254; *Sahih Muslim*, vol. 4, p. 1484, no. 6827.

كَيْفَ تَكْفُرُونَ بِٱللَّهِ وَكُنتُمْ أَمْوَٰتًا فَأَحْيَٰكُمْ ۖ
ثُمَّ يُمِيتُكُمْ ثُمَّ يُحْيِيكُمْ ثُمَّ إِلَيْهِ تُرْجَعُونَ ﴿٢٨﴾

"How can you disbelieve in Allāh and you were dead (i.e. without life) and He gave you life; then He will cause you to die, and will bring you back to life. Then to Him you will return."

He also says in verse 44 of chapter *al-Najm* (53):

وَأَنَّهُۥ هُوَ أَمَاتَ وَأَحْيَا ﴿٤٤﴾

"And that it is He who causes death and gives life."

Death then is (1) the state before life began and (2) the state in which life as we know it ceases but existence does not cease. There is an intermediary state called the *Barzakh*,[65] which occurs after visible death and before the Judgment. After the Judgment, a new and eternal life will begin.

Elsewhere in the Qur'ān, Allāh states that the fundamental purpose for which human beings were created is to worship Him:

وَمَا خَلَقْتُ ٱلْجِنَّ وَٱلْإِنسَ إِلَّا لِيَعْبُدُونِ ﴿٥٦﴾

"I only created the jinn and humankind to worship Me."
Sūrah al-Dhāriyāt (51):56

The term for worship in Arabic is *'ibādah*. In Islām, the comprehensive definition of worship is doing what pleases

[65] **"...and behind them is a *Barzakh* (barrier) until the Day when they will be resurrected."** (23:100)

worship of Allah, whatever pleases Him

Allāh and avoiding what displeases Him. Ibn Taymiyyah gave the following definition of *ʿibādah*: "*ʿibādah* is a comprehensive term that encompasses everything that Allāh loves and is pleased with, of both statements and actions, both apparent and hidden."[66] Whatever is pleasing to Allāh is good conduct. Thus, the tests of this life represent the arena in which humans worship Allāh by choosing good over evil. This is summarised in this verse as well as the following verse:

إِنَّا
جَعَلْنَا مَا عَلَى ٱلْأَرْضِ زِينَةً لَّهَا لِنَبْلُوَهُمْ أَيُّهُمْ أَحْسَنُ عَمَلًا

"Surely I[67] have created all that is on earth as its ornaments that I may test which of them is best in conduct."
Sūrah al-Kahf (18):7

Thus, the purpose for the creation of human beings in this world is expressed as a test of their conduct.[68] The creation was not for sport or jest, as Allāh stated elsewhere:

أَفَحَسِبْتُمْ أَنَّمَا خَلَقْنَٰكُمْ عَبَثًا وَأَنَّكُمْ إِلَيْنَا لَا تُرْجَعُونَ ﴿١١٥﴾

"Do you think that I created you in play [without any purpose], and that you would not be brought back to Me?"
Sūrah al-Mu'minūn (23):115

This world of life and death, wealth and poverty, sickness and health, was created to sift out the righteous souls from the evil ones. Human conduct in this world is the measure of faith.

---

[66] *Ibn Taymiyyah's Essay on Servitude* (English Translation), Al-Hidaayah Publishing, p. 29.

[67] "We" in the original Arabic is the majestic 'we', referring to God.

[68] See also chapter *Hūd*, (11):7.

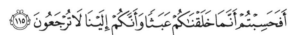

It should be noted, however, that the tests of conduct are not to inform Allāh about the actions of humankind, for He knew everything there was to know about them before He created them. The tests serve to confirm that those going to Hell on the Day of Judgment deserve it and those going to Paradise only got there by Allāh's grace. With regard to human beings in this life, the test of conduct serves two basic purposes: one, human spiritual growth, and the other, punishment or reward.

The tests of this world are primarily for the spiritual growth of human beings. Just as an intense fire separates pure gold from the rough ore to which it is bound in nature, tests purify the moral character of the believers. They force the believers to choose their higher spiritual qualities over their lower desires. Although not every test is passed, even in failure the believer grows by learning spiritual lessons to help him or her in future tests.

For example, in all human societies the qualities of generosity and contentment are considered among the most noble and admirable characteristics. However, neither of these traits can develop if everyone has the same amount of wealth. Generosity can only be acquired when the human soul — aware that sharing with the needy is good — struggles against its desire to hoard its prized possessions. Consequently, Allāh states:

لَن تَنَالُواْ ٱلْبِرَّ حَتَّىٰ تُنفِقُواْ مِمَّا تُحِبُّونَ

"You will not attain righteousness until you spend from that which you love."
Sūrah Āl-'Imrān (3):92

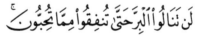

The act of forsaking what one is attached to represents the pinnacle of generosity, due to the greater difficulty involved in such a sacrifice. Thus, Allāh praises those who give of their possessions during their own time of economic difficulty. In describing actions characterising those on the straight path, Allāh states:

أَوْ إِطْعَٰمٌ فِى يَوْمٍ ذِى مَسْغَبَةٍ ﴿١٤﴾ يَتِيمًا ذَا مَقْرَبَةٍ

"(It is) giving food on a day of famine to a closely related orphan."
Sūrah al-Balad (90):14-15

He also said:

وَيُؤْثِرُونَ عَلَىٰٓ أَنفُسِهِمْ وَلَوْ كَانَ بِهِمْ خَصَاصَةٌ

"...and they gave them preference over themselves, even though they were in need."
Sūrah al-Ḥashr (59):9

Such people became worthy of Allāh's praise due to the fact that most humans are more attached to their possessions when they are scarce. It should be noted that giving away unwanted possessions is not really an expression of generosity, as many people suppose. Old possessions that are no longer used should be given away to avoid the sin of extravagance and wastage, about which Allāh said: **"Indeed the wasteful are brethren of the devils."** (17:27)

On the other hand, contentment is produced when the soul defeats the evils of envy and greed. The Creator wisely set the stage for these spiritual struggles by unequally distributing wealth in this world. Allāh says:

وَٱللَّهُ فَضَّلَ بَعْضَكُمْ عَلَىٰ بَعْضٍ فِى ٱلرِّزْقِ

"Allāh has favoured some of you over others in sustenance."
Sūrah al-Naḥl (16):71

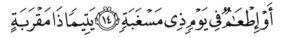

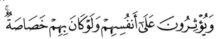

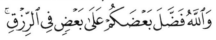

Greed and stinginess are corrupt forms of humans' natural desire to possess. The believers are informed by revelation that wealth is a trust given to humankind by Allāh. Possessions exist in the world before humans are born and remain there after they die. If wealth is used according to divine instructions, it benefits those who have it in both worlds. But if it is used selfishly, it becomes a curse in this life and a cause for punishment in the next. In chapter *al-Anfāl* of the final revelation, Allāh warns the believers to beware of the dangers of wealth and children: **"Know that your wealth and children are a test."**(8:28) Allāh further warns the believers not to let their desire for wealth and children divert them from obedience to Him, for this is the test of possessions. He says:

يَٰٓأَيُّهَا ٱلَّذِينَ ءَامَنُوا۟ لَا تُلْهِكُمْ أَمْوَٰلُكُمْ وَلَآ أَوْلَٰدُكُمْ عَن ذِكْرِ ٱللَّهِ

"O believers! Do not allow your wealth and children to divert you from the remembrance of Allāh."
Sūrah al-Munāfiqūn (63):9

وَرَفَعَ بَعْضَكُمْ فَوْقَ بَعْضٍ دَرَجَٰتٍ لِّيَبْلُوَكُمْ فِى مَآ ءَاتَىٰكُمْ

"He raised some of you over others in rank to test you with what He granted you."
Sūrah al-Anʿām (6):165

The desire to accumulate wealth cannot be satisfied in this life. The more human beings have, the more they want. The Prophet () stated that,

لَوْ أَنَّ لِٱبْنِ آدَمَ وَادِياً مِنْ ذَهَبٍ لأَحَبَّ أَنْ يَكُونَ لَهُ وَادٍ آخَرُ، وَلَا يَمْلأُ فَاهُ إلَّا
التُّرَابُ، وَيَتُوبُ اللهُ عَلَى مَنْ تَابَ

"If a man had a valley of gold, he would desire another, for nothing will fill his mouth but the dirt [of his grave]. And Allāh forgives whoever sincerely repents."[69]

This negative desire can only be overcome by the giving of one's wealth charitably. Thus, Allāh commanded the prophets to collect charity from the wealthier among their followers for distribution among the poor:

خُذْ مِنْ أَمْوَٰلِهِمْ صَدَقَةً تُطَهِّرُهُمْ وَتُزَكِّيهِم بِهَا وَصَلِّ عَلَيْهِمْ

"Take charity from their wealth to purify them and sanctify them by it, and pray for them."
Sūrah al-Tawbah (9):103

Charity was institutionalised in Islām under the Arabic name, *zakāh*[70] (compulsory charity) from its inception. Every believer with surplus wealth is obliged to give a set portion of it to the needy annually as an act of worship. *Zakāh* is one of the five pillars of Islām, and to withhold it, is considered a major sin. Giving this charity helps the believers to realise that their wealth is not their own to do with as they please. It teaches them that they are only temporary custodians of this wealth who must give a portion of it to those who are destitute. Consequently, Allāh describes true believers as those who recognise the right of the needy to a portion of their wealth.

وَفِىٓ أَمْوَٰلِهِمْ حَقٌّ لِّلسَّآئِلِ وَٱلْمَحْرُومِ ﴿١٩﴾

"And in their wealth the beggars and needy have a right."
Sūrah al-Dhāriyāt (51):19

---

[69] *Sahih Al-Bukhari*, vol. 8, pp. 297-8, no. 447.

[70] Literally *zakāh* means 'purification' and 'growth'.

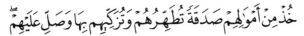

Zakāh represents basic training in generosity, wherein the believer is obliged to give away some of his or her prized possessions. However, giving in charity should be done sincerely for the pleasure of Allāh, and not for show or control of others. The reward for charity is completely lost when it is done for worldly gains. Allāh addresses this reality in chapter *al-Baqarah* as follows:

يَٰٓأَيُّهَا ٱلَّذِينَ ءَامَنُوا۟ لَا تُبْطِلُوا۟ صَدَقَٰتِكُم بِٱلْمَنِّ وَٱلْأَذَىٰ

"O believers, do not destroy your acts of charity by reminders of your generosity and by injury."
Sūrah al-Baqarah (2):264

This trains the believer to prefer and long for the eternal bliss of the hereafter over the temporary life of this world. Such a preference confirms true sincerity, a characteristic necessary for salvation. This is clearly exemplified in the following verses:

إِنَّمَا نُطْعِمُكُمْ لِوَجْهِ ٱللَّهِ لَا نُرِيدُ مِنكُمْ جَزَآءً وَلَا شُكُورًا ﴿٩﴾ إِنَّا نَخَافُ مِن
رَّبِّنَا يَوْمًا عَبُوسًا قَمْطَرِيرًا ﴿١٠﴾ فَوَقَىٰهُمُ ٱللَّهُ شَرَّ ذَٰلِكَ ٱلْيَوْمِ وَلَقَّىٰهُمْ
نَضْرَةً وَسُرُورًا ﴿١١﴾

"(They say): 'We are feeding you only for the sake of Allāh; we do not want any reward or thanks from you'...So Allāh saved them from the evil of that Day, and gave them a light of beauty and joy."
Sūrah al-Insān (76):9-11

Craving for wealth is further enhanced by envy. Consequently, Allāh also instructed us not to desire what He has given others. Allāh addresses this issue as follows:

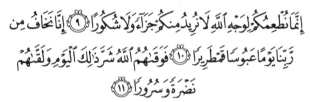

وَلَا تَتَمَنَّوْاْ مَا فَضَّلَ ٱللَّهُ بِهِۦ بَعْضَكُمْ عَلَىٰ بَعْضٍ

"Do not wish for that by which Allāh has favoured some of you over others."
Sūrah al-Nisā' (4):32

The Prophet (ﷺ) reiterated this divine piece of advice saying,

انظُرْ إلى من هو دونك، ولا تنظرْ إلى من هو فوقك، فإنه أجدرُ أن لا تزدري نعمةَ الله عندك

"Look to those less fortunate than you, and do not look to those above you; it is better for you, in order that you do not deny what Allāh has blessed you with."[71]

When human beings focus their attention on those who have more wealth than they do, envy begins to develop. They usually feel and even express that Allāh has been unfair to them. Ultimately, they may commit many sins in order to fulfil their desire for what others have. Instead, Islām advises them to consider those less fortunate than themselves. No matter how difficult circumstances may be, there are always others in more difficult situations. Consequently, reflecting on others less fortunate reminds human beings of the many bounties with which Allāh has blessed them. It is in this spiritual struggle of avoiding envy that the higher quality of contentment develops. Furthermore, according to the teachings of the prophets, material possessions do not constitute the real wealth of this world. Abū Hurayrah quoted the last Messenger (ﷺ) as saying,

---

[71] *Sahih Al-Bukhari*, vol. 8, p. 328, no. 497; and *Sahih Muslim*, vol. 4, p. 1530, no. 7070.

لَيسَ الغَنى عَن كَثرَةِ العَرَض، ولَكِنَّ الغَنى غِنى النَّفس

"Wealth is not [measured] in property, but in contentment."[72]

Being content does not mean that human beings should accept whatever circumstance they find themselves in and not try to better themselves. It means that, after striving to do one's best to achieve a good standard of living, one should accept what Allāh destines with a clear conscience. It is only by leaving one's affairs in the hands of Allāh after making an effort that the hearts find rest from the desire for the pleasures of this world.

Tests of this life also come in the form of "misfortune" and calamities, which contribute to the spiritual growth of the true believers and purify them of sin. Furthermore, misfortune reminds errant believers to return to the correct path and punishes disbelievers in this life before the next. Calamities are the foundation on which the higher spiritual quality of patience is developed. Consequently, it is not surprising to find that the righteous are subject to many tragedies and difficulties in their lives. Sa'd reported that he asked the Prophet (ﷺ) who among humankind had the most trials and he replied,

الأَنبِياءُ ثُمَّ الأَمثَلُ فالأَمثَلُ: فَيُبتَلى الرَّجُلُ عَلى حَسَبِ دِينِهِ، فَإِن كانَ في

دِينِهِ صُلبًا اشتَدَّ بَلاؤُهُ، وَإِن كانَ في دِينِهِ رِقَّةٌ ابتُلِيَ عَلى قَدرِ دِينِهِ

"The prophets, then those most like them and then those most like them. A person is tested according to the level of his faith. If his faith is firm, his

[72] *Sahih Al-Bukhari*, vol. 8, p. 304, no. 453.

trials increase in severity, and if there is weakness in his faith, he will be tried accordingly."[73]

The trials by which Allāh tests human beings are specifically tailored to their own individual needs and circumstances. Allāh creates trials for each person according to their abilities in order to bring out the best in them. It would be unfair and unjust for human beings to be tried beyond their capacities and then be punished for their failures. Consequently, Allāh emphasises in many verses of the final revelation that He is not unfair to anyone. For example, He says: **"And your Lord does not oppress anyone."**(18:49) Since Allāh is truly just, it means that the trials human beings face in this life are not beyond their ability to handle. In order to reassure humankind, Allāh states this fact repeatedly in the Qur'ān. For example, He says: **"Allāh does not burden a soul beyond its capacity."**(2:286) Furthermore, the Almighty promises that the difficult situations which humans face in life will not be without intervals of rest. If trials were continuous, they would certainly become unbearable. Consequently, every test is followed by a period of relief as Allāh emphatically states twice in chapter *al-Inshirāḥ*.

فَإِنَّ مَعَ ٱلْعُسْرِ يُسْرًا ﴿٥﴾ إِنَّ مَعَ ٱلْعُسْرِ يُسْرًا ﴿٦﴾

"For surely with difficulty comes [a period of] ease. Surely with the difficulty comes [another period of] ease."
Sūrah al-Sharḥ (94):5-6

It is due to this reality that suicide is explicitly prohibited in Islām. Allāh says:

---

[73] Collected by al-Tirmidhī and Ibn Mājah (*Sunan Ibn Majah*, vol. 5, pp. 333-4, no. 4023;); authenticated in *Ṣaḥīḥ Sunan al-Tirmidhī*, vol. 2, p. 286, no. 1956.

وَلَا تَقْتُلُوٓا۟ أَنفُسَكُمْ ۚ إِنَّ ٱللَّهَ كَانَ بِكُمْ رَحِيمًا ﴿٢٩﴾

"Do not kill yourselves, for surely Allāh is merciful with you."
Sūrah al-Nisā' (4):29

Those who commit suicide are basically saying that Allāh has burdened them beyond their capacity. They falsely accuse the Creator of treating them unfairly and thereby fall into a corrupt state of disbelief. Due to their rejection of faith, their thoughts about Allāh become evil and they fall into utter despair. 'Life,' as they often say, 'is so unfair that it is pointless to go on living.' However, Allāh said:

إِنَّهُۥ لَا يَا۟يْـَٔسُ مِن رَّوْحِ ٱللَّهِ إِلَّا ٱلْقَوْمُ ٱلْكَـٰفِرُونَ

"Surely only a disbelieving people despair of Allāh's mercy."
Sūrah Yūsuf (12):87

Consequently, Allāh has informed humankind that the punishment for those who harbour evil thoughts about Him is the eternal torment of Hell. Allāh says:

وَيُعَذِّبَ
ٱلْمُنَـٰفِقِينَ وَٱلْمُنَـٰفِقَـٰتِ وَٱلْمُشْرِكِينَ وَٱلْمُشْرِكَـٰتِ ٱلظَّآنِّينَ
بِٱللَّهِ ظَنَّ ٱلسَّوْءِ ۚ عَلَيْهِمْ دَآئِرَةُ ٱلسَّوْءِ ۖ وَغَضِبَ ٱللَّهُ عَلَيْهِمْ
وَلَعَنَهُمْ وَأَعَدَّ لَهُمْ جَهَنَّمَ ۖ وَسَآءَتْ مَصِيرًا ﴿٦﴾

"That He may punish the hypocrites, men and women, and the idolaters, men and women, who harbour evil thoughts about Allāh. An evil torment will encompass them, for Allāh is

angry with them and curses them. And He has prepared Hell for them, an evil end.”
Sūrah al-Fatḥ (48):6

On the other hand, the divine promises of justice and mercy fill the believers with the confidence necessary to patiently face the difficulties of this life. Consequently, hope in the mercy of Allāh is an essential part of faith. Those who believe in Allāh and patiently strive to do what is right, have the right to hope for His mercy, for He has promised to help and support those who are patient:

يَـٰٓأَيُّهَا ٱلَّذِينَ
ءَامَنُوا۟ ٱسْتَعِينُوا۟ بِٱلصَّبْرِ وَٱلصَّلَوٰةِ ۚ إِنَّ ٱللَّهَ مَعَ ٱلصَّـٰبِرِينَ ﴿١٥٣﴾

“O believers, seek help in patience and prayer. Truly, Allāh is with those who are patient.”
Sūrah al-Baqarah (2):153

إِنَّ ٱلَّذِينَ ءَامَنُوا۟ وَٱلَّذِينَ هَاجَرُوا۟ وَجَـٰهَدُوا۟ فِى سَبِيلِ ٱللَّهِ
أُو۟لَـٰٓئِكَ يَرْجُونَ رَحْمَتَ ٱللَّهِ ۚ وَٱللَّهُ غَفُورٌ رَّحِيمٌ ﴿٢١٨﴾

“Surely those who believed, emigrated and strove for the sake of Allāh, hope for Allāh’s mercy, for Allāh is Oft-Forgiving Most-Merciful.”
Sūrah al-Baqarah (2):218

Of course Paradise is the reward for patience based on sincere belief in Allāh. Allāh informs the believers of their reward as follows:

وَبَشِّرِ ٱلصَّـٰبِرِينَ
﴿١٥٥﴾ ٱلَّذِينَ إِذَآ أَصَـٰبَتْهُم مُّصِيبَةٌ قَالُوٓا۟ إِنَّا لِلَّهِ وَإِنَّآ إِلَيْهِ رَٰجِعُونَ

"...so announce glad tidings [of Paradise] to those who are patient. Those who, when afflicted with calamity, say: Truly we belong to Allāh and to Him we will return."
Sūrah al-Baqarah (2):155-6

Patience is also based on the belief that whatever befalls humans is fundamentally a consequence of their own evil deeds.[74] Allāh reminds humankind of this reality saying:

وَمَآ أَصَٰبَكُم مِّن مُّصِيبَةٖ فَبِمَا كَسَبَتۡ أَيۡدِيكُمۡ
وَيَعۡفُواْ عَن كَثِيرٖ ٣٠

"Whatever befalls you is a result of what your hands have earned. And He pardons much."
Sūrah al-Shūrā (42):30

The fact is that Allāh has excused humans for much of their evil. Were He to punish them strictly according to their deeds, they and all on earth would be destroyed. Allāh addresses this issue as follows:

وَلَوۡ يُؤَاخِذُ ٱللَّهُ ٱلنَّاسَ بِمَا كَسَبُواْ مَا تَرَكَ عَلَىٰ
ظَهۡرِهَا مِن دَآبَّةٖ

"And if Allāh were to punish people for what they earned, He would not leave a living creature on the face of the earth."
Sūrah Fāṭir (35):45

The practice of patience is a means to aid humankind with their trials and to help them grow spiritually. It reflects one's level of faith. Therefore, the believers are ordered to practically implement this virtue. A famous student of the

---

[74] In fact, all of the corruption on earth is a product of human misdeeds. Allāh states that in chapter *al-Rūm*, (30):41.

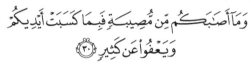

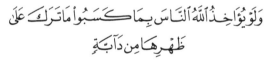

Prophet's companions, Sa'īd ibn Jubayr, was reported to have said, "Patience is an expression of a servant's recognition that what has befallen him is from Allāh, his belief that it was preordained by Him, and his anticipation of a reward for his steadfastness. A man may be frightened, but he remains steadfast and only endurance shows on him."[75] Patience is not a mere concept, but an attitude, demeanour, and specific code of behaviour defined in the Qur'ān and Sunnah. For example, the Prophet (ﷺ) advised us to say the following whenever a calamity befalls us:

إِنَّا لِلّٰهِ وَإِنَّا إِلَيْهِ رَاجِعُونَ، اللَّهُمَّ أْجُرْنِي فِي مُصِيبَتِي وَأَخْلِفْ لِي خَيْرًا مِنْهَا

(Innā lillāhi wa innā ilayhi rāji'ūn. Allāhumma ajurnī fī muṣībatī wakhluf-lī khayram minhā)

"Truly we belong to Allāh and to Him we will return. O Allāh! Recompense me in my calamity and exchange it for me with something better."[76]

This supplication serves to remind the afflicted individual that his life will come to an end and that He will return to Allāh for judgment. Viewing this world as something temporary creates an attitude in the believer that reduces the impact of the calamity. In addition, Hudhayfah ibn al-Yamān narrated, "Whenever the Prophet (ﷺ) went through some sort of affliction, he would resort to *ṣalāh* (prayer)."[77] 'Uyaynah ibn 'Abdul-Raḥmān reported that his father related that once while Ibn 'Abbās was travelling, he was informed of

[75] *Tafsir Ibn Kathir*, vol. 1, p. 127.

[76] *Sahih Muslim*, vol. 2, pp. 435-56, no. 1999.

[77] *Al-Durr al-Manthūr*, vol. 1, p. 67; also with a slightly different wording in *Sunan Abu Dawud*, vol. 1, p. 347, no. 1314; authenticated in *Ṣaḥīḥ Sunan Abū Dāwūd*, vol. 1, p. 245, no. 1171.

his brother's death. He replied, "Truly to Allāh we belong and to Him we will return." Then he went to the side of the road and prayed two units of prayer, in which he spent a long time sitting. He then walked back to his camel while reciting the verse: **"Seek help in patience and prayer. Truly it is difficult except for those who are humble."**(2:45)[78] This exemplifies the fact that true patience is practised at the time the calamity strikes and not after the initial shock wears off.

فَإِنَّ النَّبِيَّ صَلَّى اللهُ عَلَيهِ وَسَلَّمَ مَرَّ بِهَا وَهِيَ تَبكِي عِندَ قَبرٍ ، فَقَالَ : اتَّقِي
اللهَ وَاصبِرِي ، فَقَالَت : إِلَيكَ عَنِّي ، فَإِنَّكَ خِلْوٌ مِن مُصِيبَتِي ، قَالَ فَجَاوَزَهَا
وَمَضَى . فَمَرَّ بِهَا رَجُلٌ فَقَالَ : مَا قَالَ لَكِ رَسُولُ اللهِ صَلَّى اللهُ عَلَيهِ
وَسَلَّمَ؟ قَالَت : مَا عَرَفتُهُ ، قَالَ : إِنَّهُ لَرَسُولُ اللهِ صَلَّى اللهُ عَلَيهِ وَسَلَّمَ،
قَالَ : فَجَاءَت إِلَى بَابِهِ فَلَم تَجِد عَلَيهِ بَوَّاباً فَقَالَت : يَا رَسُولَ اللهِ ، وَاللهِ
مَا عَرَفتُكَ ، فَقَالَ النَّبِيُّ صَلَّى اللهُ عَلَيهِ وَسَلَّمَ : إِنَّ الصَّبرَ عِندَ أَوَّلِ صَدمَةٍ

Anas ibn Mālik narrated that once the Prophet (ﷺ) passed by a woman crying beside a grave and said to her, "Fear Allāh and be patient." She replied, "Get away from me, for you haven't been afflicted with my misfortune, and you don't even know what it is!" Someone informed her that it was the Prophet (ﷺ) [and the news struck her like death.][79] She ran to the Prophet's door, where she did not find any guard, and called out,

---

[78] *Tafsir Ibn Kathir*, vol. 1, p. 128.

[79] This addition is in the narration of *Ṣaḥīḥ Muslim*.

"Messenger of Allāh, truly I didn't know it was you." The Prophet (ﷺ) replied, "True patience is with the first shock."[80]

Demonstrating patience has many virtues and rewards. Allāh stated:

إِنَّمَا يُوَفَّى ٱلصَّٰبِرُونَ أَجْرَهُم بِغَيْرِ حِسَابٍ ﴿١٠﴾

"Only those who are patient will receive their full reward without reckoning."
Sūrah al-Zumar (39):10

In addition to the promise of Paradise, Allāh also promises to bestow His mercy, blessings, and guidance upon those who are patient. He said:

وَبَشِّرِ ٱلصَّٰبِرِينَ
﴿١٥٥﴾ ٱلَّذِينَ إِذَآ أَصَٰبَتْهُم مُّصِيبَةٌ قَالُوٓا۟ إِنَّا لِلَّهِ وَإِنَّآ إِلَيْهِ رَٰجِعُونَ
﴿١٥٦﴾ أُو۟لَٰٓئِكَ عَلَيْهِمْ صَلَوَٰتٌ مِّن رَّبِّهِمْ وَرَحْمَةٌ ۖ وَأُو۟لَٰٓئِكَ
هُمُ ٱلْمُهْتَدُونَ ﴿١٥٧﴾

"...so announce glad tidings [of Paradise] to those who are patient. Those who, when afflicted with calamity, say: 'Truly we belong to Allāh and to Him we will return.' They are the ones who will receive blessings and mercy from their Lord, and they are the guided ones."
Sūrah al-Baqarah (2):155-6

Patience can be negated by several actions:
Firstly, complaining to other people about one's trial negates

---

[80] *Sahih Al-Bukhari*, vol. 2, p. 208, no. 372; *Sahih Muslim*, vol. 2, p. 439, no. 2013; *Sunan Abu Dawud*, vol. 2, p. 890, no. 3118; *Sunan Ibn Majah*, vol. 2, p. 446, no. 1596; and *Mishkāt Al-Maṣābīḥ*, vol. 1, p. 341. The wording is from *Sunan Ibn Mājah*, vol. 2, p. 452, no. 1605.

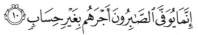

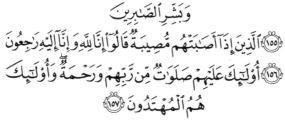

patience because, in doing so, one is in fact complaining about Allāh's divine decree. This also includes statements such as "Why me?" and "It's not fair!" This complies with the Muslims' belief that everyone will be held to account for every word they say. Thus, the concept of "venting", a concept widely advocated in today's society as a "healthy" practice, is in fact un-Islamic. However, telling others about one's trial in order to attain advice is valid. Also, complaining of one's sadness to Allāh is permitted, and may even serve to strengthen the person's relationship with Allāh. Evidence of this sanction can be found in the statement of Prophet Ya'qūb quoted in the Qur'ān.

قَالَ إِنَّمَآ أَشۡكُواْ بَثِّي وَحُزۡنِيٓ إِلَى ٱللَّهِ

"He said, 'I only complain of my sorrow to Allāh..."
Sūrah Yūsuf (12):86

Secondly, patience is negated by wailing, for the Prophet (ﷺ) said that it is indicative of disbelief.[81] Crying, however, is allowed, based on the Prophet's statement,

تَدْمَعُ الْعَيْنُ ، وَيَحْزَنُ الْقَلْبُ وَلَا نَقُولُ إِلَّا مَا يُرْضِي رَبَّنَا عَزَّ وَجَلَّ

"Indeed the eyes become full with tears and the heart feels sorrow, but we only say that which pleases our Lord."[82]

Thirdly, hitting oneself, tearing one's clothes, and other practices of self-punishment and destruction negate patience, and are strictly forbidden. Such practices are especially common in some Arab cultures. Ibn Mas'ūd reported that the Prophet (ﷺ) said,

---

[81] *Sahih Muslim*, vol. 1, p. 44, no. 128.

[82] Reported by Anas ibn Mālik; *Sahih Al-Bukhari*, vol. 2, pp. 219-20, no. 390; *Sahih Muslim*, vol. 4, p. 1243, no. 5733; *Sunan Abu Dawud*, vol. 2, p. 891, no. 3120; *Mishkāt Al-Maṣābīḥ*, vol. 1, p. 360.

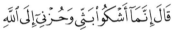

لَيْسَ مِنَّا مَنْ لَطَمَ الْخُدُودَ، وَشَقَّ الْجُيُوبَ، وَدَعَا بِدَعْوَى الْجَاهِلِيَّةِ

"Whoever slaps his face, tears his clothes, or invites (others) to an un-Islamic slogan is not of us."[83]

Fourthly, general despair is forbidden, based on the Qur'ānic verse, **"Indeed, only the disbelieving people despair of Allāh's mercy."** (12:87) Signs of despair may include "quitting" life and one's regular activities, isolating oneself completely, or falling into long term depression. Such behavioural patterns indicate a lack of faith in Allāh's promise that each hardship is followed by ease.[84]

Consequently, both the trials of good and the tests of evil benefit the believer. The lives of the true believers are balanced between the extremes of human behaviour. They neither become so happy with life's successes that they forget Allāh, nor do they become so depressed with life's difficulties and failures that they lose hope in Allāh. Instead, they remember their Lord and Benefactor's statement: **"Perhaps you may dislike something and it is good for you"** (2:216); and they trust in His decisions. Ṣuhayb ibn Sinān related that the Messenger of Allāh (ﷺ) said,

عَجَباً لأَمْرِ الْمُؤْمِنِ. إِنَّ أَمْرَهُ كُلَّهُ خَيْرٌ. وَلَيْسَ ذَاكَ لأَحَدٍ إِلاَّ لِلْمُؤْمِنِ

إِنْ أَصَابَتْهُ سَرَّاءُ شَكَرَ. فَكَانَ خَيْراً لَهُ. وَإِنْ أَصَابَتْهُ ضَرَّاءُ صَبَرَ، فَكَانَ

خَيْراً لَهُ

---

[83] *Sahih Al-Bukhari*, vol. 2, p. 216, no. 385; *Sahih Muslim*, vol. 1, p. 59, no. 184; *Sunan Ibn Majah*, vol. 2, p. 438, no. 1584; and *Mishkāt Al-Maṣābīḥ*, vol. 1, p. 361.

[84] *Sūrah al-Inshirāḥ* (94):5-6.

> *"The affair of the believer is amazing! The whole of his life is beneficial, and that is only in the case of the believer. When good times come to him, he is thankful and it is good for him, and when bad times befall him, he is patient and it is also good for him."*[85]

This is the state of one who has accepted Allāh's destiny. Consequently, belief in both the good and the apparent evil of what has been destined is the sixth pillar of faith in Islām.

Trials and calamities also purify the true believers from sin. Abū Sa'īd al-Khudrī and Abū Hurayrah reported Allāh's Messenger (ﷺ) as saying,

ما يصيبُ المُسلمَ من نَصَبٍ ولا وَصَبٍ ولا همٍّ ولا حزنٍ ولا أذىً ولا غمٍّ
حتّى الشوكةِ يُشاكها، إلّا كفّر اللهُ بها من خطاياه

> *"No fatigue, disease, sorrow, sadness, hurt, or distress befalls a Muslim – even if he were pricked by a thorn – except that Allāh expiates some of his sins by it."*[86]

On the other hand, if the believers experience a life devoid of any problems, it should be taken as a sign that something is wrong. Under such circumstances, the true believer must take time out and reflect on the realities of his or her life. Either the tests are not obvious and he is unaware of them, or he has deviated from the right path. Allāh informs the believers in *Sūrah al-Tawbah* that the apparent enjoyment which the disbelievers take from their great wealth and children is only a prelude to their punishment. He said:

---

[85] *Sahih Muslim*, vol. 4, p. 1541, no. 7138.

[86] *Sahih Al-Bukhari*, vol. 7, pp. 371-2, no. 545.

وَلَا تُعْجِبْكَ أَمْوَٰلُهُمْ وَأَوْلَٰدُهُمْ ۚ إِنَّمَا يُرِيدُ ٱللَّهُ أَن يُعَذِّبَهُم
بِهَا فِى ٱلدُّنْيَا وَتَزْهَقَ أَنفُسُهُمْ وَهُمْ كَٰفِرُونَ ﴿٨٥﴾

"Do not be awed by their wealth or their children. Allāh only wishes to punish them with these things in this life and allow their souls to die while they are in a state of disbelief."
Sūrah al-Tawbah (9):85

This is not to say that the believers should yearn for problems and calamities in their lives, for Allāh has taught them to pray:

رَبَّنَا وَلَا تَحْمِلْ عَلَيْنَآ إِصْرًا كَمَا حَمَلْتَهُۥ عَلَى ٱلَّذِينَ
مِن قَبْلِنَا ۚ

"Our Lord, do not put on us a burden like what you placed on those before us."
Sūrah al-Baqarah (2)286

Instead, they should thank Allāh for whatever trials He has spared them. However, in times of ease they must remain vigilant and not become oblivious to tests, for success and happiness often blind people to the trials of life.

Tests sometimes serve as a punishing reminder to those who have gone astray and an encouragement for them to return to the correct path. When people deviate, they seldom listen to the advice of those around them. However, when a calamity strikes them or those near and dear to them, it jolts those who still have some faith into recognising their error:

وَلَنُذِيقَنَّهُم مِّنَ ٱلْعَذَابِ ٱلْأَدْنَىٰ دُونَ ٱلْعَذَابِ ٱلْأَكْبَرِ
لَعَلَّهُمْ يَرْجِعُونَ ﴿٢١﴾

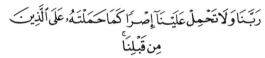

"I will make them taste a lesser punishment before the greater punishment so that perhaps they may return [to the right path]."
Sūrah al-Sajdah (32):21

The calamities which remind humankind of their deviation may come in the form of people's inhumanity to fellow humans. Modern examples include the case of the unspeakable atrocities unleashed by the Serbs against the Bosnian Muslims who had strayed far away from Islām, or Saddam's brutal invasion of Kuwait and America's subsequent indiscriminate bombing of civilian targets in Iraq. Allāh points out that some of what humans suffer at the hands of other humans; they brought upon themselves. However, the suffering is a reminder to return to the path of righteousness:

ظَهَرَ ٱلْفَسَادُ فِى ٱلْبَرِّ وَٱلْبَحْرِ بِمَا كَسَبَتْ
أَيْدِى ٱلنَّاسِ لِيُذِيقَهُم بَعْضَ ٱلَّذِى عَمِلُوا۟ لَعَلَّهُمْ يَرْجِعُونَ ﴿٤١﴾

"Corruption has appeared on the land and in the sea because of what people's hands have earned, in order that [Allāh] may make them taste a part of what they have done, and in order that they may return [to the right path]."
Sūrah al-Rūm (30):41

Calamities also serve to expose those who falsely claim faith, as well as show that those who disbelieve choose Hell by their own free will. There have been many cases of people converting to Islām for the wrong reasons, and after finding more difficulties in their lives than prior to their conversion they revert to their former beliefs. Allāh states:

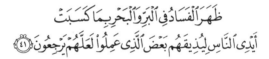

أَحَسِبَ ٱلنَّاسُ أَن يُتْرَكُوٓا۟ أَن يَقُولُوٓا۟ ءَامَنَّا وَهُمْ لَا يُفْتَنُونَ ﴿٢﴾
وَلَقَدْ فَتَنَّا ٱلَّذِينَ مِن قَبْلِهِمْ ۖ فَلَيَعْلَمَنَّ ٱللَّهُ ٱلَّذِينَ صَدَقُوا۟ وَلَيَعْلَمَنَّ
ٱلْكَٰذِبِينَ ﴿٣﴾

"Do people imagine that they will be left alone and not tested with affliction because they say, 'We believe'? Indeed, I have tested those before you. Allāh will know those who are truthful and those who lie."
Sūrah 'Ankabūt (29):2-3

Those who transgress the limits set by Allāh expose themselves to punishment in this life and the next. Throughout the Qur'ān, Allāh describes numerous past nations who rejected divine guidance and were subsequently destroyed. These stories serve to warn humankind of the consequences of rebellion against the commandments of God. In *Sūrah al-Nūr*, Allāh gives a general warning as follows:

فَلْيَحْذَرِ ٱلَّذِينَ يُخَالِفُونَ عَنْ أَمْرِهِۦٓ أَن تُصِيبَهُمْ فِتْنَةٌ
أَوْ يُصِيبَهُمْ عَذَابٌ أَلِيمٌ ﴿٦٣﴾

"Let those who contradict his command beware of a trial or a severe punishment."
Sūrah al-Nūr (24):63

The punishment may come in a variety of different ways. Perhaps the most obvious punishment afflicting humankind in all countries today is the disease AIDS,[87] which appeared for the first time in medical history in the beginning of the

[87] Acquired Immune Deficiency Syndrome (AIDS) is a condition transmitted by a virus which attacks the body's system of defense against disease, leaving the sufferer extremely vulnerable to disease and likely to die eventually from any one that he or she catches. (*Chambers Pocket Dictionary*, p. 19).

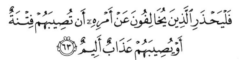

80's.[88] The vast majority of those who are affected by it around the globe are the promiscuous. Initially, homosexuals were the main victims, then bisexuals, followed by promiscuous heterosexuals and intravenous drug users. All of these groups were in open rebellion against the divine laws which restrict sexual relations to males and females within the bounds of marriage and those laws that prohibit the use of intoxicants. Some may point out that AIDS was also spread to chaste individuals through blood transfusions and to children by their parents. However, medical statistics show that such cases are relatively few in comparison to the other categories. In any case, Allāh has warned in chapter *al-Anfāl* of the final revelation that when His punishment comes it is not limited to the evil, but affects the society as a whole.

وَٱتَّقُوا۟ فِتْنَةً لَّا تُصِيبَنَّ ٱلَّذِينَ ظَلَمُوا۟
مِنكُمْ خَآصَّةً وَٱعْلَمُوٓا۟ أَنَّ ٱللَّهَ شَدِيدُ ٱلْعِقَابِ ﴿٢٥﴾

"Beware of a trial which will not afflict only the sinful among you, and know that Allāh is severe in punishment."
Sūrah al-Anfāl (8):25

One thousand four hundred years ago Prophet Muḥammad (ﷺ) prophesied the coming of such a trial. Ibn 'Umar quoted him as saying,

لَمْ تَظْهَرِ الْفَاحِشَةُ فِي قَوْمٍ قَطُّ، حَتَّى يُعْلِنُوا بِهَا، إِلَّا فَشَا فِيهِمُ الطَّاعُونُ
وَالْأَوْجَاعُ الَّتِي لَمْ تَكُنْ مَضَتْ فِي أَسْلَافِهِمُ الَّذِينَ مَضَوْا

[88] It was first identified in 1981. (*The New Encyclopaedia Britannica*, vol. 10, p. 676.)

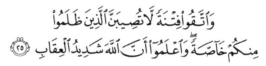

"Whenever promiscuity is openly practised among a people, a plague and anguish will spread among them which was unknown to their predecessors."[89]

However, AIDS is only one in a series of diseases. Before AIDS, a warning came in the form of another disease called herpes which became widespread among the sexually promiscuous in the 1960s and 70s. It was declared an epidemic in America in the mid-seventies, and there is no known cure for it until today. People's attention switched from it by the end of the 70s because it was not fatal,[90] while AIDS is.[91]

Allāh closes off the second verse by referring to another pair of His attributes: the All-Mighty, the Oft-Forgiving. On one hand, Allāh reminds us that creation and judgment are expressions of His invincible might and power. On the other hand, in spite of being dominant over all His creatures, He forgives anyone who repents after disobeying His instructions. The Prophet (ﷺ) quoted Allāh as saying,

إِنَّ رَحْمَتِي غَلَبَتْ غَضَبِي

"Indeed, My mercy precedes My anger."[92]

[89] *Sunan Ibn Majah*, vol. 5, pp. 331-2, no. 4019; authenticated in *Ṣaḥīḥ Sunan Ibn Mājah*, vol. 2, p. 370, no. 3246.

[90] When symptoms occur, fever and malaise are followed by burning pain in the genital area and enlargement of the lymph nodes in the groin. Blisters and small ulcers are usually found in the area of infection, and there is severe pain and burning upon urination. (*The New Encyclopaedia Britannica*, vol. 21, p. 536.)

[91] *The Purpose of Creation*, pp. 69-96.

[92] *Sahih Al-Bukhari*, vol. 9, p. 382-3, no. 519; *Sahih Muslim*, vol. 4, p. 1437, no. 6626.

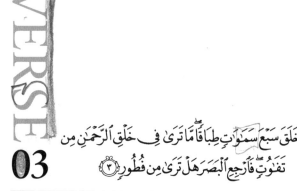

VERSE 03

ٱلَّذِى خَلَقَ سَبْعَ سَمَٰوَٰتٍ طِبَاقًا مَّا تَرَىٰ فِى خَلْقِ ٱلرَّحْمَٰنِ مِن
تَفَٰوُتٍ فَٱرْجِعِ ٱلْبَصَرَ هَلْ تَرَىٰ مِن فُطُورٍ ﴿٣﴾

miracle

sky is pure, perfect, no faults

Who has created the seven heavens one above another; you can see no fault in the creation of the Most Gracious. Then look again: "Can you see any rifts?"

The descriptions of Allāh's creations continues. After describing life and death, both of which occupy human reflection, He addresses the greatest of the creation observable to all humans, the sky, about which He said elsewhere:

لَخَلْقُ ٱلسَّمَٰوَٰتِ وَٱلْأَرْضِ أَكْبَرُ مِنْ
خَلْقِ ٱلنَّاسِ وَلَٰكِنَّ أَكْثَرَ ٱلنَّاسِ لَا يَعْلَمُونَ ﴿٥٧﴾

"Indeed, the creation of the heavens and the earth is greater than the creation of mankind, but most of mankind do not realise it."
Sūrah Ghāfir (40):57

He created the seven heavens one above another. The term *samā'* ("heaven" or "sky") is applied to anything that is spread like a canopy above any other thing.[93] Thus, the visible skies, which stretch like a vault above the earth forming a canopy, are called *samā'*. The fact that Allāh tells humankind that they will not observe any defects in it indicates that the sky must be visible to humans. That is, that it is not the "seven heavens" mentioned in the *ḥadīths* describing Prophet Muḥammad's night ascension (*mi'rāj*) to the heavens. It only refers to the lowest heaven, which is the sky of this world visible to us.

Allāh also refers to the fact that there are seven earths. He stated:

ٱللَّهُ ٱلَّذِى خَلَقَ سَبْعَ سَمَٰوَٰتٍ وَمِنَ ٱلْأَرْضِ مِثْلَهُنَّ

"It is Allāh who has created sevens heavens and of the earth the like thereof (i.e. seven)."
Sūrah al-Ṭalāq (65):12

Salīm's father narrated that the Prophet (ﷺ) said,

مَنْ أَخَذَ شِبْراً مِنَ الأَرْضِ ظُلْماً فَإِنَّهُ يُطَوَّقُهُ يَوْمَ القِيَامَةِ مِنْ سَبْعِ أَرَضِينَ

"Any person who takes a piece of land unjustly will sink down the seven earths on the Day of Resurrection."[94]

The discovery of the orbits of the planets in our solar system, the orbit of our planetary system along with countless others within our galaxy, and the movement of our galaxy along with the other galaxies through space, all confirm the universal harmony of creation.

---

[93] *Arabic-English Lexicon*, vol. 1, p. 1434.

[94] See *Sahih Al Bukhari*, vol. 4, pp. 280-1, no. 418.

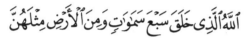

After telling humankind that they will not find any disproportion (*tafāwut*) in the skies, Allāh asks them to look again for cracks. What is being stressed here is the perfection of Allāh's creation. This verse is part of a general call for humankind to observe and reflect on their surroundings. Reflection on the perfection of creation leads most intellectual people to realise the existence of a creator, and the necessity of a purpose for creation. Observing the meticulous and deliberate nature in which the world has been fashioned causes one to become more cognizant of God and realise that this perfect design could not have been created in vain. Reflection leads people to subject themselves before Allāh, upon realising their own insignificance. The humility which results from this is essential for the establishment of God-consciousness within the individual. Allāh describes the resulting attitude and reward of those who took the time to reflect, referring to them as people of understanding. He said, **"Indeed in the creation of the heavens and the earth, and in the alteration of night and day, there are signs for people of understanding. Those who remember Allāh standing, sitting, and lying down on their sides, and who think deeply about the creation of the heavens and the earth, [saying]: 'Our Lord! You have not created all of this without purpose. Glory be to You! Give us salvation from the torment of the Fire. Our Lord! Indeed we have heard the call of one calling us to faith: Believe in your Lord! So we have believed. Our Lord! So forgive our sins, erase our evil deeds, and make us die in a state of righteousness...So their Lord responded [to their supplications, saying]: I will never allow the work of any of you to be lost, whether male or female..."** (3:190-5)

The occasion on which these verses were revealed is indeed a very touching one. 'Aṭā' related that once he and 'Ubayd ibn 'Umayr visited 'Ā'ishah. 'Ubayd said to her, *"Tell us about the most amazing thing you've witnessed from Allāh's Messenger (ﷺ)." She began crying then said, "He got up to pray [the night prayers] one night and said, 'O 'Ā'ishah, leave me to worship my Lord.' I replied, 'Indeed, I love your closeness and I also love whatever makes you happy.' So he got up and [performed ablution] then stood to pray. He started crying and continued crying until he wet his chest [with his tears]. Then he cried some more and kept crying until the floor became wet [by his tears]. Then Bilāl came to call him to prayer, and when he saw him crying, he said, 'Messenger of Allāh, you're crying while all of your past and future sins have already been forgiven?' He replied, 'Shouldn't I be a thankful slave? Indeed some verses were revealed to me tonight, and woe to whoever reads them but doesn't reflect on them:* ***"Indeed in the creation of the heavens and the earth..."'"***[95]

[95] Collected by Ibn Ḥibbān in his *Ṣaḥīḥ*, vol. 2, p. 386, no. 620; authenticated in *al-Silsilah al-Ṣaḥīḥah*, vol. 1, pp. 106-7, no. 68.

VERSE 04

ثُمَّ ٱرْجِعِ ٱلْبَصَرَ كَرَّتَيْنِ يَنقَلِبْ إِلَيْكَ ٱلْبَصَرُ خَاسِئًا وَهُوَ حَسِيرٌ ﴿٤﴾

Then look again and yet again, your sight will return to you in a state of humiliation and worn out.

you'll be emba-rrassed because nothing is wrong, it's perfect

Allāh invites humankind to look at the skies as many times as they wish and assures them that they will fail to find any disharmony or flaws in them. Fine details are often missed the first or second time that humans scrutinise an object. Consequently, Allāh does not want human beings to have any doubt whatsoever regarding the total harmony of the skies by looking until they are tired of looking. Even what is now known to modern astronomers as "black holes" cannot accurately be described as rifts in the universe. Black hole is only a name which humans have given to a phenomenon which they have no explanations for.[96] The bigger and more sophisticated that telescopes become,[97] and the farther they are able to see into the universe, the more inexplicable discoveries they make. Astronomical theories change annually, and human beings are only scratching the surface.

---

[96] A black hole is a hypothetical cosmic body of extremely intense gravity from which nothing, not even light, can escape. A black hole can be formed by the death of a massive star (those of more than three solar masses). Stars with a smaller amount of mass evolve into less compressed bodies, either white dwarfs or neutron stars. Many investigators believe that one of the component stars of the binary X-ray system Cygnus X-1 is a black hole. Discovered in 1971 in the constellation Cygnus, this binary consists of a blue supergiant and an invisible companion star that revolve about one another in a period of 5.6 days. (*The New Encyclopaedia Britannica*, vol. 2, p. 255.)

[97] E.g., the Hubble telescope is in a satellite orbiting the earth.

VERSE 05

وَلَقَدۡ زَيَّنَّا ٱلسَّمَآءَ ٱلدُّنۡيَا بِمَصَٰبِيحَ وَجَعَلۡنَٰهَا رُجُومٗا لِّلشَّيَٰطِينِۖ
وَأَعۡتَدۡنَا لَهُمۡ عَذَابَ ٱلسَّعِيرِ ٥

And indeed I have adorned the nearest heaven with lamps, and I have made such lamps (as) missiles to drive away the devils, and have prepared for them the torment of the blazing Fire.

Allāh reminds humankind that when He created the skies, He did not leave them dark and desolate, but instead, He decorated the sky closest to the world of humankind with stars. These stars resemble lamps in windows of houses in a town during a moonless night. Their lights twinkle like priceless jewels, which never cease to amaze all who gaze at them.

He further informs the believers that some of the star-like objects are used to drive the evil *jinn* away from the lower heavens. Abū Qatādah mentioned this verse then stated, "*The creation of these stars is for three purposes: decoration of the (nearest) heaven, missiles to hit the devils, and signs to guide travellers. So if anybody tries to find a different interpretation, he is mistaken and just wastes his efforts and troubles himself with what is beyond his limited knowledge.*"[98] In *Sūrah al-Jinn*, Allāh also addressed this phenomenon by describing the *jinn's* statements as follows:

وَأَنَّا لَمَسْنَا ٱلسَّمَآءَ فَوَجَدْنَٰهَا مُلِئَتْ حَرَسًا شَدِيدًا وَشُهُبًا
﴿٨﴾ وَأَنَّا كُنَّا نَقْعُدُ مِنْهَا مَقَٰعِدَ لِلسَّمْعِ ۖ فَمَن يَسْتَمِعِ ٱلْـَٔانَ
يَجِدْ لَهُۥ شِهَابًا رَّصَدًا ﴿٩﴾

"And we have sought to reach the heavens, but found it filled with stern guards and flaming fires. And indeed we used to sit there in stations to steal a hearing, but any who listens now will find a flaming fire waiting to ambush him."
Sūrah al-Jinn (72):8-9

Also, in *Sūrah al-Ḥijr*:

وَلَقَدْ جَعَلْنَا فِى ٱلسَّمَآءِ بُرُوجًا وَزَيَّنَّٰهَا لِلنَّٰظِرِينَ ﴿١٦﴾
وَحَفِظْنَٰهَا مِن كُلِّ شَيْطَٰنٍ رَّجِيمٍ ﴿١٧﴾

"And indeed, I have put the constellations in the heaven and I beautified it for the beholders. And I have guarded [the heaven] from every outcast devil. Except him that gains hearing by stealing, he is pursued by a clear, flaming fire."
Sūrah al-Ḥijr (15):16-17

---

[98] *Sahih Al-Bukhari*, vol. 4, p. 282.

This information is not conjecture or fables, it is true knowledge of the unseen which Allāh has chosen to reveal to His creatures in the final scripture, the Qur'ān. It is information about the world of the *jinn* which affects the human world.

Human beings cannot gain control over the *jinn*, as this was a special miracle given only to Prophet Sulaymān. In fact, contact with the *jinn* in circumstances other than possession or accident is most often made by the performance of sacrilegious acts despised and forbidden in the religion.[99] The evil *jinn* summoned in this fashion may aid their partners in sin and disbelief in Allāh. Their goal is to draw as many others as they can into the gravest of sins: the worship of others besides or along with God. Once fortune-tellers make contact and contract with the *jinn*, the *jinn* may inform them of certain events in the future. The Prophet (ﷺ) described how the *jinn* gather information about the future. He related that some of the *jinn* are able to travel to the lower reaches of the heavens and listen in on some of the information about the future that the angels pass among themselves. The *jinn* would then return to the earth and feed the information to their contacts.[100] This used to occur frequently prior to the prophethood of Muḥammad (ﷺ). Consequently, pre-Islamic fortune-tellers were often very accurate in their predictions. They were able to gain positions in the royal courts and enjoyed much popularity, so much so, that they were even worshipped in some religions of the world.

After the Prophet Muḥammad (ﷺ) began his mission, the situation changed. Allāh had the angels guard the lower reaches of the heavens carefully, and most of the *jinn* were chased away with meteors and shooting stars. The Prophet's companion, Ibn ʿAbbās, said, "When the Prophet (ﷺ) and a

---

[99] *Ibn Taymiyyah's Essay on the Jinn*, p. 21.

[100] *Sahih Muslim*, vol. 4, p. 1210, no. 5538.

group of his companions set out for the 'Ukāẓ market, the devils were blocked from hearing information in the heavens. Meteors were let loose on them, so they returned to their people. When their people asked what happened, they told them. Some suggested that something must have happened, so they spread out over the earth seeking the cause. Some of them came across the Prophet (ﷺ) and his companions while they were in prayer and they heard the Qur'ān. They said to themselves that this must have been what blocked them from listening. When they returned to their people they told them, **'Indeed we have heard a marvellous Qur'ān. It guides unto righteousness so we believed in it. And we will never make partners with our Lord.'**"[101] Thus, the *jinn* could no longer gather information about the future as easily as they could before the Prophet's mission. Because of that, they now mix their information with many lies. The Prophet (ﷺ) said:

ثُمَّ يُلْقِيهَا الآخَرُ إِلَى مَنْ تَحْتَهُ حَتَّى يُلْقِيهَا عَلَى لِسَانِ السَّاحِرِ أَوِ الكَاهِنِ

فَرُبَّمَا أَدْرَكَ الشِّهَابُ قَبْلَ أَنْ يُلْقِيَهَا ، وَرُبَّمَا أَلْقَاهَا قَبْلَ أَنْ يُدْرِكَهُ فَيَكْذِبُ مَعَهَا

مِائَةَ كَذْبَةٍ

"They (the jinn) would pass the information back down until it reached the lips of a magician or fortune-teller. Sometimes a meteor would overtake them before they could pass it on. If they passed it on before being struck, they would add a hundred lies to it." [102]

---

[101] *Sūrah al-Jinn* 72:1-2. The *ḥadīth* can be found in *Sahih Al-Bukhari*, vol. 6, pp. 415-16, no. 443, and *Sahih Muslim*, vol. 1, pp. 243-44, no. 908. It was also collected by al-Tirmidhī and Aḥmad.

[102] *Sahih Al-Bukhari*, vol. 8, p. 150, no. 2320; also collected by al-Tirmidhī.

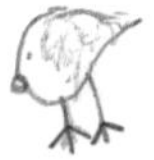

'Ā'ishah, wife of the Prophet (ﷺ), reported that when she asked him about fortune-tellers, he replied that they were nothing. She then mentioned that the fortune-tellers sometimes told things which were true. The Prophet (ﷺ) said:

تِلْكَ الْكَلِمَةُ مِنَ الْحَقِّ يَخْطَفُهَا الْجِنِّيُّ فَيَقُرُّهَا فِي أُذُنِ وَلِيِّهِ، فَيَخْلِطُونَ مَعَهَا

مِائَةَ كَذِبَةٍ

"That is a bit of truth which the jinn steals and cackles in the ear of his friend; but he mixes a hundred lies along with it."[103]

The fact that humans cannot see meteors or comets striking the *jinn* does not mean that the phenomenon does not take place. Even the origin of meteors and comets remain unknown until this day. However, there are a number of theories currently circulating among astronomers, the most popular of which is the theory that meteoroids originate from asteroids and comets. However, they admit that there are many meteoroids whose asteroidal or cometary nature remains highly uncertain.[104]

Allāh closes verse five with the warning that He has prepared a terrible punishment for the evil *jinn* and those humans who work and engage in such practices with them. Allāh stated:

---

[103] *Sahih Al-Bukhari*, vol. 7, p. 439, no. 657; and *Sahih Muslim*, vol. 4, p. 1209, no. 5535. See *The Fundamentals of Tawheed*, pp. 79-82.

[104] *The New Encyclopaedia Britannica*, vol. 27, pp. 591-2.

وَيَوْمَ يَحْشُرُهُمْ جَمِيعًا
يَٰمَعْشَرَ ٱلْجِنِّ قَدِ ٱسْتَكْثَرْتُم مِّنَ ٱلْإِنسِ ۖ وَقَالَ أَوْلِيَآؤُهُم
مِّنَ ٱلْإِنسِ رَبَّنَا ٱسْتَمْتَعَ بَعْضُنَا بِبَعْضٍ وَبَلَغْنَآ أَجَلَنَا ٱلَّذِىٓ
أَجَّلْتَ لَنَا ۚ قَالَ ٱلنَّارُ مَثْوَىٰكُمْ خَٰلِدِينَ فِيهَآ إِلَّا مَا شَآءَ ٱللَّهُ ۗ إِنَّ
رَبَّكَ حَكِيمٌ عَلِيمٌ ﴿١٢٨﴾

"One day He will gather them all together (and say), 'O assembly of jinn! You misled many humans.' Their helpers from among the humans will say, 'Our Lord! We gained benefit from one another, but now we have reached our appointed term which You appointed for us!" He will say: 'The Fire will be your dwelling-place, and you will dwell therein forever, except as Allāh may will..."

Sūrah al-Anʿām (6):128

Consequently, not only are the evil *jinns* destroyed by shooting stars in this life, but in the next life they will suffer an even greater torment.

VERSE

* characteristics of Hell
* categories of Kufr

06 وَلِلَّذِينَ كَفَرُوا۟ بِرَبِّهِمْ عَذَابُ جَهَنَّمَ ۖ وَبِئْسَ ٱلْمَصِيرُ ﴿٦﴾

And for those who disbelieve in their Lord (Allāh) is the torment of Hell; an awful destination.

Because of the sacrilege and heresy involved in fortune-telling, Islām has taken a very strong stance towards it. Islām opposes any form of association with those who practise fortune-telling, except to advise them to give up their forbidden practices. The Prophet (ﷺ) laid down principles which clearly forbade any form of visitation of fortune-tellers. Ṣafiyyah reported from Ḥafṣah, the wife of the Prophet (ﷺ), that the Prophet (ﷺ) said,

من أتى عرافا فسأله عن شيء لم تقبل له صلاة أربعين ليلة

"The ṣalāh of whoever approaches a fortune-teller and asks him about anything will not be accepted for 40 days and nights."[105]

---

[105] *Sahih Muslim*, vol. 4, p. 1211, no. 5540.

The punishment in this tradition is for simply approaching a fortune-teller and asking him questions out of curiosity. This prohibition is further supported by Muʿāwiyah ibn al-Ḥakam al-Salamī's report in which he said, "Messenger of Allāh, verily there are some people among us who visit oracles." The Prophet (ﷺ) replied, *"Do not go to them."*[106] Such a severe punishment has been assigned for only visitation because it is the first step to belief in fortune-telling. If one went there doubtful about its reality, and some of the fortune-teller's predictions come true, one is likely to become a true devotee of the fortune-teller and an ardent believer in fortune-telling.

The individual who approaches a fortune-teller is still obliged to make his compulsory prayers throughout the 40 day period, even though he gets no reward from his prayers. If he abandons the prayer altogether, he has committed an even greater sin. Whenever obligatory prayer is performed, it produces two results under normal circumstances: (1) It removes the obligation of that prayer from the individual, and (2) It earns him a reward. Consequently, though the reward is lost for 40 days, the obligation still remains.

The Islamic ruling regarding anyone who visits a fortune-teller, believing that he knows the unseen and the future, is that of *Kufr* (disbelief). Abū Hurayrah reported from the Prophet (ﷺ) that he said,

مَنْ أَتَى كَاهِنًا أَوْ عَرَّافًا فَصَدَّقَهُ بِمَا يَقُولُ، فَقَدْ كَفَرَ بِمَا أُنْزِلَ عَلَى مُحَمَّدٍ صَلَّى اللهُ عَلَيْهِ وَسَلَّمَ

"Whosoever approaches a fortune-teller and believes what he says has disbelieved in what was revealed to Muḥammad."[107]

---

[106] Ibid., p. 1209, no. 5532.

[107] *Sunan Abu Dawud*, vol. 2, p. 1095, no. 3895; authenticated in *Ṣaḥīḥ Sunan Abū Dāwūd*, vol. 2, p. 732, no. 3304; also collected by Aḥmad and al-Bayhaqī.

Belief in fortune-tellers assigns to creation some of Allāh's attributes with regard to knowledge of the unseen and the future. Consequently, it destroys faith in the Unique Oneness of Allāh (*tawḥīd*) and represents a form of idolatry (*shirk*). The ruling of *Kufr* includes, by analogy (*qiyās*), those who read the books and writings of fortune-tellers, listen to them on the radio, watch them on the television, or find them in computer programs, as these are the most common means used by 20th century fortune-tellers to spread their predictions. Therefore, all the various methods used around the world by oracles, fortune-tellers and the like are forbidden to Muslims. These methods include palm-reading, I-Ching, fortune cookies, tea leaves as well as horoscopes and Bio-rhythm computer programs, as they all claim to inform those who believe in them about their future. Allāh has stated in no uncertain terms that He alone knows the future:

إِنَّ ٱللَّهَ عِندَهُۥ عِلۡمُ ٱلسَّاعَةِ وَيُنَزِّلُ ٱلۡغَيۡثَ
وَيَعۡلَمُ مَا فِي ٱلۡأَرۡحَامِۖ وَمَا تَدۡرِي نَفۡسٞ مَّاذَا تَكۡسِبُ غَدٗاۖ
وَمَا تَدۡرِي نَفۡسُۢ بِأَيِّ أَرۡضٖ تَمُوتُۚ إِنَّ ٱللَّهَ عَلِيمٌ خَبِيرُۢ ٣٤

"Certainly the knowledge of the Hour is with Allāh alone. It is He who sends down the rain and knows the contents of the wombs. No one knows what he will earn tomorrow nor in which land he will die, but Allāh is All-Knowing and Aware."

Sūrah Luqmān (31):34

Therefore, Muslims must take utmost care in dealing with books, magazines, newspapers as well as individuals who, in one way or another, claim knowledge of the future or the unseen. For example, when a Muslim weatherman predicts rain, snow, or other climatic conditions for the future, he should add the phrase, "*Inshā' Allāh* (If Allāh so wishes)." Likewise, when the Muslim doctor informs her patient that she will deliver a child in 9 months or on such and such a day, she should take care to add the phrase '*Inshā' Allāh*', as such statements are only estimations based on statistical information.[108]

The Categories of Kufr

Disbelief (*kufr*) may be divided into two main categories with regard to its effect on the person's status in the religion.

1. Major *Kufr* that removes one who does it or believes in it from the religion.

2. Minor *Kufr* that does not remove one from the religion.

Major Kufr

Major *Kufr* has been divided by some scholars into six main categories according to the way in which the disbelief takes place.

1. Outright Rejection (*takdhīb*)

This form of *kufr* may be defined as disbelief with the tongue and heart that leads to open rejection of the message.

وَيَوْمَ نَحْشُرُ مِن كُلِّ أُمَّةٍ فَوْجًا مِّمَّن يُكَذِّبُ بِـَٔايَٰتِنَا فَهُمْ
يُوزَعُونَ ﴿٨٣﴾ حَتَّىٰٓ إِذَا جَآءُو قَالَ أَكَذَّبْتُم بِـَٔايَٰتِى
وَلَمْ تُحِيطُوا۟ بِهَا عِلْمًا

"The Day when I will gather from every nation a group of those who rejected My signs, they

[108] *The Fundamentals of Tawheed*, pp. 84-87.

will be driven until they come [before their Lord] and He asks: Did you reject My signs even though you did not completely know them?"

Sūrah al-Naml, (27):83-4

2. Denial (*juḥūd*)

In this case of *kufr*, the person's belief is hidden by outward vocal denial of what is known to be the truth.

وَجَحَدُوا۟ بِهَا وَٱسْتَيْقَنَتْهَآ أَنفُسُهُمْ ظُلْمًا وَعُلُوًّا

"And they denied them wrongly and arrogantly while their souls were certain of them."

Sūrah al-Naml, (27):14

3. Obstinance (*'inād*)

This type of *kufr* refers to one who believes both outwardly and inwardly, but rejects the message due to anger, arrogance, pride, etc. Iblīs and Abū Ṭālib are examples of this type of disbelief.

إِلَّآ إِبْلِيسَ أَبَىٰ وَٱسْتَكْبَرَ وَكَانَ مِنَ ٱلْكَـٰفِرِينَ

"... except Iblīs who proudly refused and became one of the disbelievers."

Sūrah al-Baqarah, (2):34

أَلْقِيَا فِى جَهَنَّمَ كُلَّ كَفَّارٍ عَنِيدٍ ﴿٢٤﴾

"Throw into Hell every stubborn disbeliever."

Sūrah Qāf, (50):24

4. Avoidance (*iʿrāḍ*)

Disbelief of this type addresses the *kufr* of those who ignore and avoid the message out of arrogance or carelessness. This is the disbelief of those who do not even want to hear the message because they are too busy with their lives.

كِتَٰبٌ فُصِّلَتْ ءَايَٰتُهُۥ قُرْءَانًا عَرَبِيًّا لِّقَوْمٍ يَعْلَمُونَ ﴿٣﴾
بَشِيرًا وَنَذِيرًا فَأَعْرَضَ أَكْثَرُهُمْ فَهُمْ لَا يَسْمَعُونَ ﴿٤﴾

"A Book whose verses are explained in detail; an Arabic Qur'ān for people who know. As a giver of good tidings and a warner but most of them shun it and refuse to listen."
Sūrah Fuṣṣilat, (41):3-4

5. Hypocrisy (*nifāq*)

This type of disbelief refers to those who outwardly express belief and conform to many or most of the prescribed practices while inwardly they harbour disbelief.

إِنَّ ٱلْمُنَٰفِقِينَ فِى ٱلدَّرْكِ ٱلْأَسْفَلِ مِنَ ٱلنَّارِ

"Indeed the hypocrites will be in the lowest levels of the Hellfire."
Sūrah al-Nisā', (4):145

6. Doubt (*shakk*)

Hesitation and doubt about the message is the basis of this type of disbelief.[109] A modern example of this type of *kufr* is the disbelief of the agnostic who says: "I don't know enough to form a definite opinion about the existence or non-existence of God or the Hereafter. I guess I'll find out when I get there.

---

[109] See *The Fundamentals of Takfir*, pp. 2-16.

وَدَخَلَ جَنَّتَهُۥ وَهُوَ ظَالِمٌ لِّنَفْسِهِۦ قَالَ مَآ أَظُنُّ أَن تَبِيدَ هَٰذِهِۦٓ
أَبَدًا ﴿٣٥﴾ وَمَآ أَظُنُّ ٱلسَّاعَةَ قَآئِمَةً وَلَئِن رُّدِدتُّ إِلَىٰ رَبِّى
لَأَجِدَنَّ خَيْرًا مِّنْهَا مُنقَلَبًا ﴿٣٦﴾

"He went into his garden in a state of self oppression saying, 'I don't think this will ever disappear nor do I think the Hour will ever come. And even if I am brought back to my Lord, I will surely find something better."

Sūrah al-Kahf, (18):35-6

Disbelief which expels a person from Islām may occur in thought, statement or act.

1. Disbelief in thought includes any belief of *shirk* about Allāh, or attributing deficiency to Him, or belief in the permissibility of fornication or consumption of intoxicants, etc.

2. Stated disbelief includes cursing or ridiculing Allāh and His Messenger, etc., whether done seriously or in jest.

3. Acts of disbelief which constitute the opposite of faith and remove the doer from Islām include acts like prostration to idols or graves, and acts of sacrilege like spitting on the Qur'ān, etc..

Minor Kufr

Minor *Kufr* includes acts of disobedience which have been defined as *kufr* by Allāh and His Messenger (ﷺ) which are done without being accompanied by the belief that they are lawful. This type of disbelief is also referred to as *Kufr 'Amalī* (disbelief in action) as distinct from *Kufr I'tiqādī* (disbelief in faith) which removes one who commits it from the religion.

An example of acts defined as *kufr* by Allāh can be found in the following verse:

وَمَن لَّمْ يَحْكُم بِمَآ أَنزَلَ ٱللَّهُ فَأُو۟لَٰٓئِكَ هُمُ ٱلْكَٰفِرُونَ ﴿٤٤﴾

"And whoever does not judge by what Allāh revealed are disbelievers."
Sūrah al-Mā'idah, (5):44

Ṭāwūs quoted Ibn ʿAbbās as saying, "It is disbelief less than disbelief.[110] He has committed an act of disbelief, but he is not like one who disbelieves in Allāh, His angels, His books, His messengers and the hereafter."[111] ʿAlī ibn Abī Ṭalḥah[112] related from Ibn ʿAbbās that he said, "Whoever rejects what was revealed by Allāh has disbelieved. Whoever accepts it, yet does not judge by it is a sinner [*fāsiq*]."[113] Ibn Masʿūd and al-Ḥasan both said, "[This verse] refers in general to all who do not judge by what Allāh revealed, believing in it and making it permissible."[114]

Examples from the *Sunnah* can be found in the following authentic statements of the Prophet (ﷺ):

Ibn Masʿūd quoted the Prophet (ﷺ) as saying,

سِبَابُ الْمُسْلِمِ فُسُوقٌ وَقِتَالُهُ كُفْرٌ

"Cursing a Muslim is sinful and fighting him is disbelief."[115]

---

[110] Collected by Ibn al-Mundhir and al-Ḥākim (2:313).

[111] Collected by al-Marwazī (2:521) and Ibn Jarīr (10:356).

[112] ʿAlī ibn Abī Ṭalḥah was a student of Ibn ʿAbbās' students, ʿIkrimah and Mujāhid. He is considered one of the most authentic routes to the *Tafsīr* of Ibn ʿAbbās.

[113] *Tafsīr al-Ṭabarī*

[114] *Al-Jāmi' li Aḥkām al-Qur'ān*, vol. 6, p. 190.

[115] *Sahih Al-Bukhari* and *Sahih Muslim*

He also said,

اثْنَانِ هُمَا كُفْرٌ : النِّيَاحَةُ ، وَالطَّعْنُ فِي النَّسَبِ

"Two things in people are disbelief: speaking ill about another's lineage and wailing over the dead."[116]

Ibn 'Umar related that he heard the Prophet (ﷺ) say,

مَنْ حَلَفَ بِغَيْرِ اللهِ فَقَدْ أَشْرَكَ

"Whoever makes an oath by other than Allāh has committed an act of disbelief."[117]

لَا تَرْغَبُوا عَنْ آبَائِكُمْ . فَمَنْ رَغِبَ عَنْ أَبِيهِ فَهُوَ كُفْرٌ

"Don't curse your fathers. Whoever curses his father has committed an act of disbelief."[118]

مَنْ أَتَى حَائِضاً أَوِ امْرَأَةً فِي دُبُرِهَا أَوْ كَاهِناً : فَقَدْ كَفَرَ بِمَا أُنْزِلَ عَلَى مُحَمَّدٍ

"Whoever has sex with a menstruating woman or enters a woman from her anus, or goes to a fortune-teller has disbelieved in what was revealed to Muḥammad."[119]

Ibn al-Qayyim said, "If a person judged according to other than what Allāh revealed, or did something that Allāh's Messenger (ﷺ) called *kufr* while adhering to Islām and it's legislation, he has done both *kufr* and Islām. Furthermore, it is clear that every kind of sin is a branch of *kufr*, just as every

---

[116] *Sahih Muslim*

[117] Collected by Abū Dāwūd and al-Tirmidhī

[118] *Sahih Al-Bukhari* and *Sahih Muslim*

[119] Collected by the authors of the four *Sunan*

act of obedience is a branch of *īmān* (faith). Doing a branch of *īmān* may be called believing, though the person doing it may not be called a believer. Similarly committing an act of disbelief is called *kufr* but the label should not be applied absolutely to those who commit it."[120]

The relationship between kufr and shirk

Although *kufr* and *shirk* are not the same, they are interrelated. It is commonly held that although every form of *shirk* is *kufr*, not every form of *kufr* is *shirk*. However, some scholars were of the opinion that the two words were synonymous; that every form of *kufr* is a form of *shirk*. Verse 48 from *Sūrah al-Nisā'* (4) is quoted as evidence that they are the same: **"Indeed Allāh will not forgive that partners be given to Him, but He can forgive less than that for whomsoever He wishes."** The following *ḥadīth* is also cited as evidence: Mu'āwiyah quoted Allāh's Messenger as saying,

كُلُّ ذَنْبٍ عَسَى اللهُ أَنْ يَغْفِرَهُ إِلَّا الرَّجُلُ يَمُوتُ كَافِرًا أَوِ الرَّجُلُ يَقْتُلُ مُؤْمِنًا مُتَعَمِّدًا

"Perhaps Allāh will forgive every sin except that of a man who dies in disbelief and one who kills a believer intentionally."[121]

However, it could be said that their end is one and the same, but that doesn't make their sin the same.

Atheists commit *shirk* by attributing creation to chance and their desires become their god when it comes to deciding what is right and wrong. A recent manifestation of *shirk* among

---

[120] *Al-Ṣalāh*, by Ibn al-Qayyim

[121] Collected by Aḥmad and al-Nasā'ī and authenticated in *Silsilah al-Aḥādīth al-Ṣaḥīḥah*, no. 511.

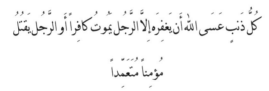

scientists and environmentalists is the Gaia hypothesis, put forward by James Lovelock and Lynn Margulies. They claim that the earth is alive; it is a single entity and every living thing is a part of it. The name Gaia is from the ancient Greek name for the Earth Goddess. Naturally, this idea is very attractive to radical feminists as well. It reminds one of *Sūrah al-Nisā'* (4):117: "**They worship in place of Him only females. However, they are only praying to Satan, a rebel.**"

Jews commit *shirk* by taking their rabbis as lords in place of Allāh and Buddhism, which is officially an atheist religion, as popularly practicsed, involves worship of the image of the Buddha.

Atheists, members of some other religions, and some modern sects of Christianity which deny the existence of Hell often raise the question as to why a loving and merciful God would create Hell and burn some of His creatures in it eternally. Heaven and Hell are the reward and punishment, respectively, for deeds in this life. Abū Hurayrah reported that Allāh's Messenger (ﷺ) said,

احْتَجَّتِ النَّارُ وَالْجَنَّةُ . فَقَالَتْ هَذِهِ : يَدْخُلُنِي الْجَبَّارُونَ وَالْمُتَكَبِّرُونَ

وَقَالَتْ هَذِهِ : يَدْخُلُنِي الضُّعَفَاءُ وَالْمَسَاكِينُ . فَقَالَ اللّٰهُ ، عَزَّ وَجَلَّ ، لِهَذِهِ

أَنْتِ عَذَابِي أُعَذِّبُ بِكِ مَنْ أَشَاءُ وَرُبَّمَا قَالَ : أُصِيبُ بِكِ مَنْ أَشَاءُ . وَقَالَ

لِهَذِهِ : أَنْتِ رَحْمَتِي أَرْحَمُ بِكِ مَنْ أَشَاءُ ، وَلِكُلِّ وَاحِدَةٍ مِنْكُمَا مِلْؤُهَا

"There was a dispute between Hell and Paradise, during which Hell said, 'The haughty and the proud will find abode in me.' Then Paradise said, 'The meek and the humble will find their abode in me.' Then Allāh, the Exalted and Glorious, said (to Hell): 'You are (the means) of My punishment

by which I punish those of My servants whom I wish.' And He said (to Paradise): 'You are My Mercy by means of which I will show mercy to those whom I wish. And each one of you will be full.'"[122]

Allāh is loving and merciful, as is manifest in the Prophet's statement,

لَوْ لَمْ تُذْنِبُوا لَذَهَبَ اللهُ بِكُمْ، وَلَجَاءَ بِقَوْمٍ يُذْنِبُونَ، فَيَسْتَغْفِرُونَ اللهَ، فَيَغْفِرُ لَهُمْ

"If you did not commit sins and turn to Allāh seeking His forgiveness, He would have replaced you with another people who would sin and ask Allāh's forgiveness, and He would forgive them."[123]

Every one of the 114 chapters of the final revelation, except one,[124] begins with the statement, *"In the name of Allāh, the Beneficent, the Most Merciful."* Allāh's attributes of mercy and forgiveness are stressed to encourage humans not to fall into despair. No matter how great the sins of a person may be, Allāh can forgive them if he turns back to Him in sincere repentance. Allāh said:

۞ قُلْ يَـٰعِبَادِيَ ٱلَّذِينَ أَسْرَفُوا۟ عَلَىٰٓ أَنفُسِهِمْ لَا تَقْنَطُوا۟ مِن رَّحْمَةِ ٱللَّهِ إِنَّ ٱللَّهَ يَغْفِرُ ٱلذُّنُوبَ جَمِيعًا إِنَّهُۥ هُوَ ٱلْغَفُورُ ٱلرَّحِيمُ

"Say: O My slaves who have transgressed against themselves, do not despair of Allāh's

---

[122] *Sahih Muslim*, vol. 4, pp. 1482-3, no. 6818.

[123] *Sahih Muslim*, vol. 4, pp. 1435-6, no. 6621; reported by Abū Ayyūb al-Ansārī.

[124] *Sūrah al-Tawbah* (9).

Mercy. Indeed, Allāh forgives all sins. Truly, He is the Most Forgiving, the Most Merciful.”
Sūrah al-Zumar (39):53

The Messenger (ﷺ) was quoted as saying,

إِنَّ اللّٰهَ لَمَّا قَضَى الْخَلْقَ كَتَبَ عِنْدَهُ فَوْقَ عَرْشِهِ إِنَّ رَحْمَتِي سَبَقَتْ غَضَبِي

“When Allāh created the universe, He made an obligation on Himself [recorded] in a document kept by Him: My mercy precedes my wrath.”[125]

He was also reported to have said,

إِنَّ لِلّٰهِ مِائَةَ رَحْمَةٍ . أَنْزَلَ مِنْهَا رَحْمَةً وَاحِدَةً بَيْنَ الْجِنِّ وَالْإِنْسِ وَالْبَهَائِمِ وَالْهَوَامِّ فَبِهَا يَتَعَاطَفُونَ . وَبِهَا يَتَرَاحَمُونَ . وَبِهَا تَعْطِفُ الْوَحْشُ عَلَى وَلَدِهَا . وَأَخَّرَ اللّٰهُ تِسْعًا وَتِسْعِينَ رَحْمَةً . يَرْحَمُ بِهَا عِبَادَهُ يَوْمَ الْقِيَامَةِ

“[Allāh created] mercy with one hundred parts, one of which was sent down upon the jinn, human beings and other living beings. It is out of this one part that they love each other, show kindness to each other and even the animals treat their offspring with affection. Allāh has reserved the remaining ninety-nine parts for His true worshippers on the Day of Resurrection.”[126]

However, Allāh’s attributes of mercy and love have to be considered in the context of His justice. Were He to put the evil and corrupt disbelievers in Paradise along with the righteous believers, it would be unjust. His instructions of righteousness

[125] *Sahih Muslim*, vol. 4, p. 1437, no. 6628; reported by Abū Hurayrah.

[126] Ibid., vol. 4, p. 1437, no. 6631; reported by Abū Hurayrah.

in this life would become meaningless if the reward were the same for both. There would have been no need for prophets and revelation if belief and disbelief were equal. They are not, as He states:

أَفَمَن كَانَ مُؤْمِنًا كَمَن كَانَ فَاسِقًا ۚ لَّا يَسْتَوُۥنَ ﴿١٨﴾

"Is he who is a believer like him who is a disobedient disbeliever? No. They are not equal."
Sūrah al-Sajdah (32):18

VERSE 07

إِذَآ أُلۡقُواْ فِيهَا سَمِعُواْ لَهَا شَهِيقٗا وَهِيَ تَفُورُ ٧

When they are thrown inside, they will hear the (terrible) drawing in of its breath as it blazes forth.

The disbelievers will hear the Hellfire inhale (*shahīq*) as they fall in and are sucked into its core. At the same time, its flames will gush out to meet and surround them. They will be boiled in fire like a few peas in a large amount of water.[127] In this verse, Allāh describes the Hellfire as a creature which inhales, and in *Sūrah al-Furqān* He describes it as one which exhales:

إِذَا رَأَتۡهُم مِّن مَّكَانِۭ بَعِيدٖ سَمِعُواْ لَهَا تَغَيُّظٗا وَزَفِيرٗا ١٢

"When Hell sees them from a far place, they will hear its raging and its roaring (zafīr)."
Sūrah al-Furqān (25):12

Allāh also describes it as speaking on the Day of Judgment after people are thrown in.

---

[127] This is the explanation of Imām al-Thawrī as quoted by Ibn Kathīr (*Tafsīr al-Qur'ān al-'Aẓīm*, vol. 4, p. 423).

يَوْمَ نَقُولُ لِجَهَنَّمَ هَلِ ٱمْتَلَأْتِ وَتَقُولُ هَلْ مِن مَّزِيدٍ ﴿٣٠﴾

"One day I will ask Hell, 'Are you full?' and it will answer, 'Is there any more?'"
Sūrah Qāf (50):30

Anas ibn Mālik reported that Allāh's Messenger (ﷺ) said,

يُلقَى فِي النَّارِ وتقولُ هل من مزيدٍ ، حتّى يضعَ قدمهُ فتقولُ : قطْ قطْ

"The people will be thrown into the Fire and it will say, 'Is there any more?' until Allāh will place His foot over it. It will then say, 'Enough! Enough!'"[128]

ʿAbdullāh ibn Masʿūd quoted Allāh's Messenger (ﷺ) as saying,

يؤتى بجهنم يومئذٍ لها سبعونَ ألفَ زمامٍ . مع كلِّ زمامٍ سبعونَ ألفَ ملكٍ يجرُّونها

"Hell will be brought on that day having seventy thousand reins with seventy thousand angels drawing each rein."[129]

In many verses throughout the Qur'ān, Allāh describes the torment of the Hellfire in detail. He describes that its flames **"burn away right to the skull"** (70:16), and how its inhabitants will experience no brief breaks or moments of relief. He says:

كُلَّمَا نَضِجَتْ جُلُودُهُم بَدَّلْنَٰهُمْ جُلُودًا غَيْرَهَا لِيَذُوقُوا۟ ٱلْعَذَابَ ۗ

[128] *Sahih Al-Bukhari*, vol. 6, p. 353, no. 371.

[129] *Sahih Muslim*, vol. 4, p. 1482, no. 6810.

"As often as their skins are roasted through, I (Allāh) will exchange them for other skins so that they may taste the punishment."
Sūrah al-Nisā' (4):56

Its food and drink are described as **"boiling fluid, a filthy fluid of pus, blood, and other penalties of a similar kind to match them."** (38:57-8). Its inhabitants will also eat from the tree of *Zaqqūm*, which is **"a tree that springs out of the bottom of the Hellfire. The shoot of its fruit-stalks are like the heads of devils."** (37:64-5)

It must be noted that the disbelievers will not be the only ones tasting the torment of the Hellfire. Although Muslims will eventually go to Paradise, they may spend some time before that in Hell as a punishment for sins they did not repent for in this life, unless Allāh forgives them. Hence, Muslims should reflect on the realities of the Hellfire and its horrendous tortures, as opposed to viewing it as a remote concept. One of the reasons which the Companions of the Prophet (ﷺ) attained such high levels of righteousness was their attitude toward the verses of the Qur'ān. They applied the meanings of the verses to themselves, whenever applicable, before pointing fingers at others. Today, Muslims tend to brush off verses about the Hellfire, with a quick assumption that it does not apply to them, but applies to others instead. However, if we read about the Hellfire and reflect on its vivid descriptions, knowing that we may experience its punishment if we are not repentant, our *taqwā* (God-consciousness, fear of Allāh) will increase, by Allāh's will. That is, its descriptions should cause us to strive harder to please Allāh in every aspect of our lives and to turn to Him in sincere repentance whenever we sin.

VERSE 08

تَكَادُ تَمَيَّزُ
مِنَ ٱلْغَيْظِ ۖ كُلَّمَآ أُلْقِىَ فِيهَا فَوْجٌ سَأَلَهُمْ خَزَنَتُهَآ أَلَمْ يَأْتِكُمْ نَذِيرٌ ﴿٨﴾

It almost bursts apart with fury. Every time a group is cast inside it, its keepers will ask: "Did no warner come to you?"

The fury of the Hellfire will be so great that it almost explodes. As the disbelievers are thrown in, the angels guarding the Hellfire will mock them for being there.[130] Allāh describes these angels as being stern and severe:

عَلَيْهَا مَلَٰٓئِكَةٌ غِلَاظٌ شِدَادٌ لَّا يَعْصُونَ ٱللَّهَ مَآ أَمَرَهُمْ
وَيَفْعَلُونَ مَا يُؤْمَرُونَ ﴿٦﴾

"...over it are angels stern and severe, who do not disobey the commands they receive from Allāh, but do whatever they are commanded."
Sūrah al-Taḥrīm (66):6

[130] *Tafsīr al-Sa'dī*, vol. 5, p. 266.

Because their job is not a pleasant one, they have to be harsh. They are not allowed any sympathy for those assigned to Hell who will beg and plead with them for mercy. Their number is identified in the Qur'ān as follows:

عَلَيۡهَا تِسۡعَةَ عَشَرَ ﴿٣٠﴾ وَمَا جَعَلۡنَآ أَصۡحَٰبَ ٱلنَّارِ إِلَّا مَلَٰٓئِكَةٗۙ
وَمَا جَعَلۡنَا عِدَّتَهُمۡ إِلَّا فِتۡنَةٗ لِّلَّذِينَ كَفَرُواْ

"Over it are nineteen. And I have only appointed angels as guardians of the fire and fixed their number as a trial for the disbelievers..."

Sūrah al-Muddaththir (74):30-31

In *Sūrah al-Zukhruf*, the name of the main guardian is given as "Mālik":

وَنَادَوۡاْ يَٰمَٰلِكُ لِيَقۡضِ عَلَيۡنَا رَبُّكَۖ قَالَ إِنَّكُم مَّٰكِثُونَ ﴿٧٧﴾

"They will cry out: 'O Mālik, let your Lord put an end to us!' He will reply, 'Surely you will stay as you are.'"

Sūrah al-Zukhruf (43):77

The guardians will mock those being thrown in because only those who were not warned should make the kind of mistakes which brought them there. The angels' question will only increase the remorse and torment which the inhabitants of Hell will experience.

VERSE 09

قَالُوا۟ بَلَىٰ قَدْ جَآءَنَا نَذِيرٌ فَكَذَّبْنَا وَقُلْنَا مَا نَزَّلَ ٱللَّهُ مِن شَىْءٍ إِنْ أَنتُمْ
إِلَّا فِى ضَلَـٰلٍ كَبِيرٍ ﴿٩﴾

They will say: "Yes indeed; a warner did come to us, but we called him a liar and said: 'Allāh has not revealed anything. You are indeed in great error.'"

Allāh relates the admissions of those going to Hell in order to demonstrate to human beings how just He is with His creation. It is His promise that He will not punish anyone until after the truth has been made clear to him or her. Allāh states this reality as follows:

وَمَا كُنَّا مُعَذِّبِينَ حَتَّىٰ نَبْعَثَ رَسُولًا ﴿١٥﴾

"I will not punish anyone until after a messenger is sent."
Sūrah al-Isrā' (17):15

However, once a messenger is sent as divine evidence, human beings are obliged to submit themselves and follow him. Abū Hurayrah narrated that the Prophet (ﷺ) said,

وَالَّذِي نَفْسُ مُحَمَّدٍ بِيَدِهِ لاَ يَسْمَعُ بِي أَحَدٌ مِنْ هَذِهِ الأُمَّةِ يَهُودِيٌّ وَلاَ نَصْرَانِيٌّ

ثُمَّ يَمُوتُ وَلَمْ يُؤْمِنْ بِالَّذِي أُرْسِلْتُ بِهِ، إِلاَّ كَانَ مِنْ أَصْحَابِ النَّارِ

"By Him in whose hand is Muḥammad's soul (i.e. Allāh), there is none among the Jews and Christians who hears about me, then dies without believing in the Message with which I've been sent, except that he will be from the dwellers of the Hellfire."[131]

Based on Allāh's infinite knowledge, He could have created all members of the human race who were to live on earth and immediately placed some of them in Paradise and the remainder in Hell. Before creating man, Allāh already knew what choices they would make in this life, what provision and opportunities He would give them, and in what state of belief or disbelief they would die. Therefore, in one sense it could be said that some people were created for Paradise and others for Hell. 'Ā'ishah, wife of the Prophet Muḥammad (ﷺ), quoted him as saying,

أَوَلاَ تَدْرِينَ أَنَّ اللهَ خَلَقَ الْجَنَّةَ وَخَلَقَ النَّارَ. فَخَلَقَ لِهَذِهِ أَهْلاً، وَلِهَذِهِ أَهْلاً

"Don't you know that Allāh created Paradise and Hell, and He created inhabitants for each?"[132]

If Allāh had immediately placed those headed for Paradise in Paradise, they would not question Allāh's decision. Those in Paradise would happily accept an everlasting life of bliss and be thankful that they were not placed in Hell. However, those immediately placed in Hell would ask why. They would feel a sense of unfairness due to their ignorance of what they

[131] *Sahih Muslim*, vol. 1, p. 91, no. 284.

[132] *Sahih Muslim*, vol. 4, p. 1400, no. 6435.

would have done had they lived on earth. Those in Hell would relentlessly argue that had they been given a chance to live out their lives on earth, they would have believed the warners sent to them and done righteous deeds. Consequently, Allāh allows human beings to live out their lives on earth and make all the choices they would have made, so that everyone who enters Hell will know that they chose Hell by themselves. They will recognise Allāh's mercy in their lives and acknowledge their sin in rejecting His signs and guidance. And they will accept His judgment as being just and beyond reproach.[133]

As to those who did not come in contact with the divine evidence due to an early death (i.e. death before the age of puberty), mental deficiency or ignorance, they will have an opportunity to choose between obeying or disobeying Allāh on the Day of Resurrection. Anas quoted Allāh's Messenger (ﷺ) as saying,

يُؤْتَى بِأَرْبَعَةٍ يَوْمَ الْقِيَامَةِ، بِالْمَوْلُودِ، وَبِالْمَعْتُوهِ، وَبِمَنْ مَاتَ فِي الْفَتْرَةِ وَالشَّيْخِ

الْفَانِي كُلُّهُمْ يَتَكَلَّمُ بِحُجَّتِهِ فَيَقُولُ الرَّبُّ تَبَارَكَ وَتَعَالَى

لِعُنُقٍ مِنَ النَّارِ ابْرُزْ. فَيَقُولُ لَهُمْ: إِنِّي كُنْتُ أَبْعَثُ إِلَى عِبَادِي رُسُلًا مِنْ

أَنْفُسِهِمْ، وَإِنِّي رَسُولُ نَفْسِي إِلَيْكُمُ ادْخُلُوا هَذِهِ، فَيَقُولُ مَنْ كُتِبَ عَلَيْهِ

الشَّقَاءُ، يَا رَبِّ أَيْنَ نَدْخُلُهَا وَمِنْهَا كُنَّا نَفِرُّ؟ قَالَ: وَمَنْ كُتِبَتْ عَلَيْهِ السَّعَادَةُ

يَمْضِي، فَيَقْتَحِمُ فِيهَا مُسْرِعًا. قَالَ فَيَقُولُ تَبَارَكَ وَتَعَالَى: أَنْتُمْ لِرُسُلِي أَشَدُّ

تَكْذِيبًا وَمَعْصِيَةً فَيَدْخُلُ هَؤُلَاءِ الْجَنَّةَ، وَهَؤُلَاءِ النَّارَ

---

[133] *The Purpose of Creation*, pp. 27-29.

"Four groups of people will be resurrected on the Day of Resurrection: the newly born, the mentally insane, those who died in the period between two messengers, and the senile. Each will present his case. Then the Lord will tell a flame from the Hellfire to come out. He will then say, 'I used to send to My slaves messengers from among themselves. Today I am My own messenger to you. So enter this fire.' Those destined for Hell will say, 'Our Lord, how can we enter it when we were supposed to escape from it?' Then the ones destined to be happy will rush forth and jump into it without hesitation. Allāh will say to those who refused, 'You would have been even more disbelieving and disobedient to My messengers.' Then the second group [i.e. those who obeyed Allāh and jumped in] will enter Paradise, and the first group will enter the Hellfire."[134]

Allāh gave the prophets miracles to convince those who denied their status. The Qur'ān remains as evidence that Allāh did reveal His word to humankind. It is fundamentally a literary miracle, which is inimitable in the Arabic original, and it contains scientific data beyond the knowledge of the time in which it was revealed.

---

[134] Collected by Abū Yaʿlā and al-Bazzār and authenticated in *Silsilah al-Aḥādīth al-Ṣaḥīḥah*, no. 2468. Narration no. 1434 is similar to it.

VERSE 10

وَقَالُوا۟ لَوْ كُنَّا نَسْمَعُ أَوْ نَعْقِلُ مَا كُنَّا فِىٓ أَصْحَـٰبِ ٱلسَّعِيرِ ۝١٠

And they will say, "If only we had listened or used our intelligence, we would not be among the dwellers of the blazing Fire!"

They will all regret and blame themselves, though it will not be of any benefit to them at that stage. If they had listened to the prophets and warners, they would have been rightly guided. Likewise, if reason and intelligence are used properly, they must lead humans to the realisation of Allāh's existence and the fact that a definite plan underlies all of His creation.[135]

It should be noted that listening is mentioned before reasoning because the pre-requisite for obtaining guidance is to listen to (or read) the teachings of the Prophet (ﷺ). To reflect on the teachings and to try to understand the truth is secondary.[136] **Without prophetic guidance, human beings cannot reach the**

[135] *The Message of the Qur'an*, p. 880, note 8.

[136] *The Meaning of the Quran*, vol. 6, pp. 14-5, note 16.

truth by themselves, using only their intellect and common sense.

Those who reject divinely organised religion take their own desires as their god, as Allāh stated:

أَرَءَيْتَ مَنِ ٱتَّخَذَ إِلَـٰهَهُۥ هَوَىٰهُ

"Haven't you seen the one who takes his desires as his god?"
Sūrah al-Furqān (25):43

Divinely revealed religion represents the guide for humankind, which the prophets of God brought. They demonstrated the righteous way of life which the Creator wanted human beings to live. It is only by following the way of the prophets that humankind can attain salvation. This is the meaning of the famous statement attributed to Prophet Jesus in the Gospel according to John 14:6: *"Jesus said to him, 'I am the way, and the truth, and the life; no one comes to the Father, but by me."*

Although those who worship Jesus commonly quote this verse as part of the evidence for his divinity, Jesus did not invite people to worship himself instead of God, or as God. If these words were indeed spoken by Jesus, what they mean is that one cannot worship Allāh except in the way defined by the prophets of Allāh. Jesus emphasised to his disciples that they could only worship Allāh using the way he had taught them. In the Qur'ān, Allāh instructs Prophet Muḥammad (ﷺ) to tell mankind to follow him if they truly love God:

قُلْ إِن كُنتُمْ تُحِبُّونَ ٱللَّهَ
فَٱتَّبِعُونِى يُحْبِبْكُمُ ٱللَّهُ وَيَغْفِرْ لَكُمْ ذُنُوبَكُمْ ۗ وَٱللَّهُ غَفُورٌ رَّحِيمٌ

"Tell [the people]: If you [really] love Allāh, then follow me, and Allāh will love you and

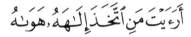

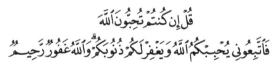

forgive your sins, for Allāh is Oft-Forgiving, Most Merciful."
Sūrah Āl-'Imrān (3):31

The way of the prophets is the only way to Allāh, because it was prescribed by Allāh Himself, and the purpose of the prophets was to convey Allāh's instructions to humankind. Without prophets, people would not know how to worship Allāh. Allāh stated:

لَّقَدْ كَانَ لَكُمْ فِي رَسُولِ ٱللَّهِ أُسْوَةٌ حَسَنَةٌ

"Surely there is for you in Allāh's Messenger an excellent example."
Sūrah al-Aḥzāb (33):21

Consequently, all prophets informed their followers of how to worship Allāh. Therefore, adding anything to the religion brought by the prophets is incorrect.

Any changes made to the religion after the time of the prophets represents deviation inspired by Satan. In this regard, Prophet Muḥammad (ﷺ) was reported to have said,

مَنْ أَحْدَثَ فِي أَمْرِنَا هَذَا مَا لَيْسَ مِنْهُ فَهُوَ رَدٌّ

"Whoever adds anything new to the religion of Islām, will have it rejected [by Allāh]."[137]

Furthermore, anyone in Jesus' time who worshipped Allāh contrary to Jesus' instructions would have worshipped in vain.

In order to understand the 'way' of Jesus, first and foremost, it must be realised that Jesus Christ, the son of Mary, was

[137] *Sahih Al-Bukhari*, vol. 3, p. 535, no. 861, and *Sahih Muslim*, vol. 3, p. 931, no. 4266.

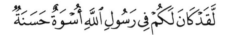

the last in the line of Jewish prophets. He lived according to the Torah, the law of Moses, and taught his followers to do likewise. In Matthew 5:17-18, the following statement has been attributed to Jesus: "**17** *Think not that I have come to abolish the law and the [way of] the prophets; I have come not to abolish them but to fulfil them.* **18** *For, I say to you, till heaven and earth pass away, not an iota, not a dot, will pass from the law until all is accomplished."* Unfortunately, about five years after the end of Jesus' ministry, a man by the name of Saul of Tarsus, who claimed to have seen Jesus in a vision, began to change Jesus' way. Paul (his Roman name) had considerable respect for Roman philosophy and he spoke proudly of his own Roman citizenship. His conviction was that non-Jews who became Christians should not be burdened with the Torah in any respect. The author of Acts 13:39 quotes Paul as saying, *"And by him everyone that believes is freed from everything from which you could not be freed by the law of Moses."* It was primarily through the efforts of Paul that the Church began to take on its non-Jewish character. Paul wrote most of the New Testament letters (epistles), which the Church accepts as the official doctrine and inspired Scripture.[138] These letters do not preserve the Gospel of Jesus or even represent it;[139] instead, Paul transformed the teachings of Christ into a Hellenic (Greco-Roman) philosophy.[140]

On the other hand, the Qur'ān was written down and memorised, from beginning to end, during the lifetime of the Prophet (ﷺ). Within a year after his death, the first standard written text was produced. And within 14 years after his death, authorised copies made from the standard codex were sent to the capitals of the Muslim state, while unauthorised copies were destroyed. Since the Prophet's death in 632 CE

---

[138] He was beheaded in Rome 34 years after the end of Jesus' ministry.

[139] *Biblical Studies From a Muslim Perspective*, p. 18.

[140] *The True Message of Jesus Christ*, pp. 85-8.

until today, an increasing number of people in each successive generation have memorised the Qur'ān from beginning to end. An orientalist scholar, John Burton, stated that the text of the Qur'ān available today is "the text which has come down to us in the form in which it was organised and approved by the Prophet...What we have today in our hands is the *mushaf* [Arabic Qur'ānic text] of Muhammad."[141] This is evidence that Allāh's promise is definitely true, for He said:

إِنَّا نَحْنُ نَزَّلْنَا ٱلذِّكْرَ وَإِنَّا لَهُۥ لَحَـٰفِظُونَ ﴿٩﴾

"Indeed I have revealed the Reminder (Qur'ān) and indeed I will preserve it."
Sūrah al-Ḥijr (15):9

However, Allāh's preservation of the Qur'ān did not stop with the actual text. The original meaning was also safeguarded by the Prophet's divinely guided explanations of the Qur'ān in speech and action. Because the *Sunnah* was based on divine guidance, it represents Allāh's promise, **"Indeed I will explain it."** (75:19) The explanations of the Qur'ān and *Sunnah* were both safeguarded by the companions of Prophet Muḥammad (ﷺ), their students, and the righteous scholars which followed them, commonly referred to as *al-salaf al-ṣāliḥ* (the pious predecessors). The Companions were present while the Qur'ān was being revealed and received their understanding directly from the Prophet's clarifications and application. Therefore, we are required to submit to their understanding of the Qur'ān and the *Sunnah*.

[141] *The Collection of the Qur'an*, p. 239-40. See *The True Message of Jesus Christ*, pp. 31-33, for more on this topic.

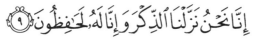

VERSE 11

فَٱعْتَرَفُوا۟ بِذَنۢبِهِمْ فَسُحْقًا لِّأَصْحَـٰبِ ٱلسَّعِيرِ ﴿١١﴾

Then they will confess their sin; so away with the dwellers of the blazing Fire.

Those sent to Hell will confess their sins hoping for some mercy; however, confession at that stage will be of no avail. Repentance wipes away sin if it is done in this life before the throes of death overcome the individual. In *Sūrah al-Nisā'* Allāh addressed this reality as follows:

وَلَيْسَتِ ٱلتَّوْبَةُ لِلَّذِينَ
يَعْمَلُونَ ٱلسَّيِّـَٔاتِ حَتَّىٰٓ إِذَا حَضَرَ أَحَدَهُمُ ٱلْمَوْتُ
قَالَ إِنِّى تُبْتُ ٱلْـَٔـٰنَ وَلَا ٱلَّذِينَ يَمُوتُونَ وَهُمْ كُفَّارٌ ۚ
أُو۟لَـٰٓئِكَ أَعْتَدْنَا لَهُمْ عَذَابًا أَلِيمًا ﴿١٨﴾

"There is no repentance for those who continue to do evil until death comes upon one of them and he says, "Indeed, I have now repented,' nor

for those who died in disbelief. I have prepared for them a most grievous punishment."
Sūrah al-Nisā' (4):18

Prophet Muḥammad (ﷺ) was reported by 'Abdullāh ibn 'Umar as saying,

إِنَّ اللهَ تَعَالَى يَقْبَلُ تَوْبَةَ عَبْدِهِ مَا لَمْ يُغَرْغِرْ

"Allāh, most Great and Glorious, will accept His servant's repentance until his death rattle begins."[142]

Repentance will also not be accepted at the end of the world when the major signs of the Last Day appear beginning with the rising of the sun in the West. At that time, declaration of faith by disbelievers will be futile. The souls of all the believers will be taken just prior to the western sunrise and only the faithless will remain alive in the world.[143] Abū Hurayrah quoted the Prophet (ﷺ) as saying,

ثَلَاثٌ إِذَا خَرَجْنَ، لَا يَنْفَعُ نَفْسًا إِيمَانُهَا لَمْ تَكُنْ آمَنَتْ مِنْ قَبْلُ أَوْ كَسَبَتْ فِي

إِيمَانِهَا خَيْرًا: طُلُوعُ الشَّمْسِ مِنْ مَغْرِبِهَا، وَالدَّجَّالُ، وَدَابَّةُ الْأَرْضِ

"When three things appear, faith will not benefit one who has not previously believed or has not derived any good from his faith; the rising of the sun from its place of setting, the Anti-Christ, and the beast of the earth."[144]

---

[142] Collected by al-Tirmidhī, Ibn Mājah, Aḥmad and Mālik and authenticated in *Ṣaḥīḥ Sunan Ibn Mājah*, vol. 2, p. 418, no. 3430. See *Riyāḍ-al-Ṣāliḥīn*, vol. 1, p. 12, no. 18 for an English translation.

[143] *Sahih Muslim*, vol. 4, p. 1506, no. 6945.

[144] *Sahih Muslim*, vol. 1, pp. 94-5, no. 296.

Consequently, this verse is a reminder to those who delay doing acts of righteousness and prefer to continue enjoying sinful pleasures. Allāh will take their souls without warning and they will not have a chance to repent. In *Sūrah al-An'ām*, Allāh warned:

فَلَمَّا
نَسُوا۟ مَا ذُكِّرُوا۟ بِهِۦ فَتَحْنَا عَلَيْهِمْ أَبْوَٰبَ كُلِّ شَىْءٍ
حَتَّىٰٓ إِذَا فَرِحُوا۟ بِمَآ أُوتُوٓا۟ أَخَذْنَٰهُم بَغْتَةً فَإِذَا هُم مُّبْلِسُونَ ﴿٤٤﴾

"So when they forgot what they were reminded of, I opened to them the gates of every pleasant thing, until in the midst of their enjoyment of what they were given, I took them suddenly in their state of confusion and regret."
Sūrah al-An'ām (6):44

VERSE 12

إِنَّ ٱلَّذِينَ يَخۡشَوۡنَ رَبَّهُم بِٱلۡغَيۡبِ لَهُم مَّغۡفِرَةٞ وَأَجۡرٞ كَبِيرٞ ۝١٢

Certainly, those who fear their Lord unseen, theirs will be forgiveness and great reward.

Fear of Allāh is not like fear of wild animals; that is, the fear of the harm they can do. When one fears the creation, he or she runs away from it and dreads meeting it. To fear the Lord is to fear His displeasure out of a great love for His pleasure. In other words, it is to love Him so intensely that one fears doing anything that displeases Him. Those believers with this consciousness refrain from acts of disobedience even when they cannot be seen by people.[145] Such intensity of love, which creates within a person a God-conscious, humble and repentant character, earns forgiveness for any past sins. Abū ʿUbaydah ibn ʿAbdillāh related that Allāh's Messenger (ﷺ) said,

التَّائِبُ مِنَ الذَّنْبِ كَمَنْ لَا ذَنْبَ لَهُ

---

[145] *Tafsīr al-Qur'ān al-ʿAẓīm*, vol. 4, p. 424.

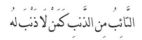

"One who repents from sin is like one without sin."[146]

Fear of Allāh includes fear of the Hellfire, crying as a result of being conscious of Allāh's presence, and crying out of remorse for not fulfilling His commandments. Our pious predecessors serve as beacons of light for us in their example of fearing Allāh. For example, ʿAbdullāh ibn Shaddād related that he would hear the sobbing of ʿUmar ibn al-Khaṭṭāb, from the last rows of prayer while he recited certain verses from the Qur'ān.[147] Abū Hurayrah narrated that Allāh's Messenger (ﷺ) said,

لَا يَلِجُ النَّارَ رَجُلٌ بَكَى مِنْ خَشْيَةِ اللهِ حَتَّى يَعُودَ اللَّبَنُ فِي الضَّرْعِ

"No person who cries out of fear of Allāh will enter Hell, until milk returns to the udder."[148]

Ibn al-Qayyim said, "It is incumbent upon every Muslim to fear Allāh. He said: **'Do not fear them, but rather fear Me, if you are indeed believers.'** (3:175). **'And you should fear only Me'** (2:40). The positive and recommended fear is that which prevents the individual from the forbidden. Fear beyond that may lead the person to despondency, which is itself forbidden."[149] Imām al-Ghazālī said, "Too much fear leads to despair and prevents good deeds. The object of fear is to give encouragement to righteous actions."[150] Allāh has stated, **"No one despairs of Allāh's Mercy except those who have no faith."** (12:87)

---

[146] *Sunan Ibn Majah*, vol. 5, p. 489, no. 4250; authenticated in *Ṣaḥīḥ Sunan Ibn Mājah*, vol. 2, p. 418, no. 3427.

[147] Bukhārī, and authenticated by Shaykh al-Albānī in *al-Mukhtaṣar*, vol. 1, p. 182.

[148] Collected by al-Tirmidhī and authenticated in *Ṣaḥīḥ Sunan al-Tirmidhī*, vol. 2, p. 267, no. 1881.

[149] *Madārij al-Sālikīn*, vol. 1, p. 548.

[150] *Iḥyā' ʿUlum-al-Dīn*, vol. 4, p. 145.

Abū Hurayrah related that the Prophet (ﷺ) said,

سَبعةٌ يُظِلُّهم اللهُ في ظلّه يومَ لا ظلَّ إلا ظلُّه : الإمامُ العادلُ ، وشابٌّ نَشأَ في عبادة ربه ، ورجلٌ قلبُه معلَّقٌ في المساجد ، ورجلان تَحابّا في الله اجتَمعا عليه وتفرَّقا عليه ، ورجلٌ طلبَتْه امرأةٌ ذاتُ منصبٍ وجمالٍ فقال : إني أخافُ الله ، ورجلٌ تَصدَّقَ أخفى حتى لا تَعلمَ شمالُه ما تُنفقُ يمينُه ورجلٌ ذكرَ اللهَ خالياً ففاضتْ عيناه

"Seven people will be shaded by Allāh on a day where there will be no other shade but His. They are:

a) a just ruler;

b) a young man who has been brought up worshipping Allāh sincerely;

c) a man whose heart is attached to the mosques;

d) two persons who love each other only for the sake of Allāh, and they meet and part company for the sake of Allāh;

e) a man who refuses the invitation of a charming woman of noble birth to engage in extra-marital sex saying, 'Indeed I fear Allāh';

f) a person who practises charity so secretly that his left hand does not know what his right hand has given;

g) a person who remembers Allāh when he is alone and his eyes become filled with tears."[151]

---

[151] *Sahih Al Bukhari*, vol. 2, pp. 289-90, no. 504.

The Prophet's wife, 'Ā'ishah, said,

سَأَلْتُ رَسُولَ اللهِ عَنْ هَذِهِ الآيَةِ ﴿ وَالَّذِينَ يُؤْتُونَ مَا آتَوْا وَقُلُوبُهُمْ وَجِلَةٌ ﴾ قَالَتْ

عَائِشَةُ : أَهُمُ الَّذِينَ يَشْرَبُونَ الْخَمْرَ وَيَسْرِقُونَ؟ قَالَ : لَا يَا بِنْتَ

الصِّدِّيقِ . وَلَكِنَّهُمُ الَّذِينَ يَصُومُونَ وَيُصَلُّونَ وَيَتَصَدَّقُونَ وَهُمْ يَخَافُونَ أَنْ لَا

تُقْبَلَ مِنْهُمْ : أُولَئِكَ الَّذِينَ يُسَارِعُونَ فِي الْخَيْرَاتِ وَهُمْ لَهَا سَابِقُونَ

"I asked Allāh's Messenger about the verse: **And those who give in charity with their hearts full of fear** *(23:60) — if they were those who drink alcohol and steal. He replied, 'No! O daughter of al-Siddīq, they are those who fast, pray, and are charitable, who fear that their good deeds may not be accepted from them (by Allāh).* **It is these who race for good deeds and are first to do them** *(23:61).'"*[152]

This is the basis of morality in religion. Those who avoid evil only because it is wrong in their opinion may change their opinion later, or may have been mistaken in their opinion. Those who avoid evil for fear of worldly loss are likely to do evil when there does not appear to be any chance of loss. Those who avoid evil for fear of punishment from the authorities will not restrain themselves when they feel that they cannot be observed or caught.

It should be noted that true fear of Allāh is based on knowledge. The more a person grows in knowledge of Allāh and His commandments, the more he or she fears Allāh. Consequently,

---

[152] *Sunan Ibn Majah*, vol. 5, p.. 460, no. 4198; authenticated in *Ṣaḥīḥ Sunan Ibn Mājah*, vol. 2, p. 409, no. 3384; also collected by al-Tirmidhī.

Allāh praised the scholars in this regard, saying: **"Those who truly fear Allāh are the scholars."** (35:28)

'Ā'ishah reported that the Prophet (ﷺ) said,

إِنَّ أَتْقَاكُمْ وَأَعْلَمَكُمْ بِاللهِ أَنَا

"By Allāh, I have more knowledge of Allāh than they do and I fear Him the most."[153]

The ultimate reward for fearing Allāh is forgiveness of sin and Paradise. In *Sūrah al-Nāzi'āt*, Allāh promises:

وَأَمَّا مَنْ خَافَ مَقَامَ رَبِّهِۦ وَنَهَى ٱلنَّفْسَ عَنِ ٱلْهَوَىٰ ﴿٤٠﴾
فَإِنَّ ٱلْجَنَّةَ هِىَ ٱلْمَأْوَىٰ ﴿٤١﴾

"As for him who feared standing before his Lord, and restrained himself from his desires and lusts, verily, Paradise will be his home."
Sūrah al-Nāzi'āt (79):40

In *Sūrah al-Raḥmān*:

وَلِمَنْ خَافَ مَقَامَ رَبِّهِۦ جَنَّتَانِ ﴿٤٦﴾

"And he who fears standing before his Lord will have two gardens in Paradise."
Sūrah al-Raḥmān (55):46

Ibn 'Abbās explained that this verse meant that one who feared standing before Allāh on the Day of Judgment will not obey his evil desires or prefer this world over the next. He will realise that the next world is better and more lasting, and therefore fulfil his duties and avoid the prohibited. Such an individual will be given two gardens in Paradise on the Day

---

[153] *Sahih Al Bukhari* vol. 9, p. 298, no. 404; and *Sahih Muslim* vol. 4, p. 1255-6, no. 5814.

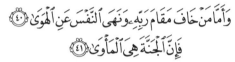

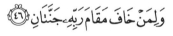

of Judgment.[154] Ibn 'Abbās' student, Mujāhid, commented that this verse refers to a person who intends to do a sin, but restrains himself due to his fear of standing before Allāh.[155]

[154] *Tafsīr al-Qur'ān al-'Aẓīm*, vol. 4, p. 296.

[155] This narration is not translated in the English version of *Sahih Al Bukhari*, vol. 6, p. 372. Ibn Ḥajar indicated that 'Abdul-Razzāq narrated it with a complete chain from Mujāhid (*Fatḥ al-Bārī*, vol. 10, p. 716).

VERSE 13

وَأَسِرُّواْ قَوْلَكُمْ أَوِ ٱجْهَرُواْ بِهِۦٓ ۖ إِنَّهُۥ عَلِيمٌۢ بِذَاتِ ٱلصُّدُورِ ﴿١٣﴾

Whether you keep your conversations secret or disclose them, He certainly knows everything in the hearts.[156]

Allāh reminds humans that He is well aware of their actions and intentions. No secrets are hidden from Him. The Prophet (ﷺ) was reported to have said,

إنّما الأعمال بالنيّات

> *"Deeds are judged according to their intentions."*[157]

Consequently, the believers are encouraged to reflect on the completeness of Allāh's knowledge in order to correct the intentions behind their words and actions. It is also essential

[156] The term '*ṣudūr*' literally means 'chests', however the intent here is hearts, where human secrets are symbolically kept. (*Tafsīr al-Qur'ān al-'Aẓīm*, vol. 4, p. 424.)

[157] *Sahih Al Bukhari*, vol. 1, p. 1, no. 1.

that conversation, whether private or public, be about good. The Messenger of Allāh (ﷺ) said,

وَمَن كَانَ يُؤْمِنُ بِاللّٰهِ وَالْيَوْمِ الْآخِرِ فَلْيَقُلْ خَيْراً أَوْ لِيَصْمُتْ

"Whoever believes in Allāh and the Last Day should either speak good or be silent."[158]

Allāh encourages the believers to avoid secret meetings. He states:

﴿لَّا خَيْرَ فِي كَثِيرٍ مِّن نَّجْوَىٰهُمْ إِلَّا مَنْ أَمَرَ بِصَدَقَةٍ
أَوْ مَعْرُوفٍ أَوْ إِصْلَٰحٍ بَيْنَ ٱلنَّاسِ ۚ وَمَن يَفْعَلْ ذَٰلِكَ
ٱبْتِغَآءَ مَرْضَاتِ ٱللَّهِ فَسَوْفَ نُؤْتِيهِ أَجْرًا عَظِيمًا ﴿١١٤﴾

"There is no good in most of their secret talks except (in talks of) one who enjoins charity, righteous deeds, or conciliation among people. And he who does this seeking Allāh's pleasure, I will give him a great reward."

Sūrah al-Nisā' (4):114

He also reminds us that He is well aware of whatever takes place in such "secret" meetings, for no secret can be kept from Him. He said:

مَا يَكُونُ مِن نَّجْوَىٰ ثَلَٰثَةٍ إِلَّا هُوَ رَابِعُهُمْ وَلَا خَمْسَةٍ إِلَّا هُوَ
سَادِسُهُمْ وَلَآ أَدْنَىٰ مِن ذَٰلِكَ وَلَآ أَكْثَرَ إِلَّا هُوَ مَعَهُمْ أَيْنَ مَا كَانُوا ۖ ثُمَّ
يُنَبِّئُهُم بِمَا عَمِلُوا يَوْمَ ٱلْقِيَٰمَةِ ۚ إِنَّ ٱللَّهَ بِكُلِّ شَيْءٍ عَلِيمٌ ﴿٧﴾

---

[158] Narrated by Abū Hurayrah and collected in *Sahih Al-Bukhari*, vol. 8, p. 29, no. 47; and *Sahih Muslim*, vol. 1, p. 32, no. 75.

"There is no secret meeting of three, except that He is their fourth (with His knowledge), nor of five, except that He is their sixth (with His knowledge), nor (any meeting) with less (people) than that or more, except that He is with them wherever they may be. Then on the Day of Resurrection He will inform them of what they did. Indeed, Allāh is, of all things, Knowing."
Sūrah al-Mujādilah (58):7

Human beings do not have complete control over their thoughts; bad thoughts may be introduced to their minds by those around them or by the media or by the evil *jinn* assigned to every individual known as the *qarīn*. Consequently, Allāh absolved his creatures of their sinful thoughts as long as they do not act upon them. Abū Hurayrah quoted the Prophet (ﷺ) as saying,

إِنَّ اللّٰهَ تَجَاوَزَ لِأُمَّتِي مَا حَدَّثَتْ بِهِ أَنْفُسَهَا مَا لَمْ يَتَكَلَّمُوا أَوْ يَعْمَلُوا بِهِ

"Allāh overlooks the evil thoughts of the Muslim Ummah (nation) as long as they do not speak about it or act on it."[159]

On the other hand, Allāh is most merciful, in that He rewards good intentions, even if the person could not do the deed, and rewards those who intended evil but refrained from doing it. Abū Hurayrah also related that Allāh's Messenger (ﷺ) said,

[159] *Sahih Al-Bukhari*, vol. 7, p. 147, no. 194; and *Sahih Muslim*, vol. 1, p. 74, no. 230.

فَمَنْ هَمَّ بِحَسَنَةٍ فَلَمْ يَعْمَلْهَا كَتَبَهَا اللَّهُ لَهُ عِنْدَهُ حَسَنَةً كَامِلَةً، فَإِنْ هُوَ هَمَّ بِهَا
فَعَمِلَهَا كَتَبَهَا اللَّهُ لَهُ عِنْدَهُ عَشْرَ حَسَنَاتٍ إِلَى سَبْعِمِائَةِ ضِعْفٍ إِلَى أَضْعَافٍ
كَثِيرَةٍ وَمَنْ هَمَّ بِسَيِّئَةٍ فَلَمْ يَعْمَلْهَا كَتَبَهَا اللَّهُ لَهُ عِنْدَهُ حَسَنَةً كَامِلَةً، فَإِنْ هُوَ هَمَّ
بِهَا فَعَمِلَهَا كَتَبَهَا اللَّهُ لَهُ سَيِّئَةً وَاحِدَةً

"Whoever intends to do a good deed and does not do it will get the reward of one good deed, but if he does it he will get from ten to seven hundred times the reward. While one who intends to do evil and does not do it will also get the reward of one good deed, but if he does it he will only have recorded against him one bad deed."[160]

[160] *Sahih Al-Bukhari*, vol. 9, pp. 437-8, no. 592; and *Sahih Muslim*, vol. 1, pp. 75-6, no. 237.

VERSE 14 أَلَا يَعْلَمُ مَنْ خَلَقَ وَهُوَ ٱللَّطِيفُ ٱلْخَبِيرُ ﴿١٤﴾

Should He Who has created not know, even though He is Most Subtle and Aware?

A logical argument is presented here in support of the completeness of God's knowledge. Could anyone in their right mind doubt that the Creator of man and his world knows the deepest and darkest of human secrets? Especially considering the fact that His will operates within His creation in imperceptible ways.

وَلَقَدْ خَلَقْنَا ٱلْإِنسَٰنَ وَنَعْلَمُ مَا تُوَسْوِسُ بِهِۦ نَفْسُهُۥ ۖ وَنَحْنُ أَقْرَبُ إِلَيْهِ
مِنْ حَبْلِ ٱلْوَرِيدِ ﴿١٦﴾

"Indeed I have created man, and I know the whisperings of his soul, for I am nearer to him than his jugular vein."
Sūrah Qāf (50):16

Combining this with the belief that Allāh is the Most Merciful, should create in a person increased trust in Allāh's judgments and divine plans.

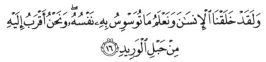

The attribute *Laṭīf* (Subtle) also means 'gentle'. Were Allāh not gentle and kind to His creatures, not a single living being would remain on the surface of the earth. He stated: **"And if Allāh were to punish people for what they earned, He would not leave a living creature on the face of the earth."**(35:45) God bestows His gifts on His creatures in ways which they are unaware of. He protects them from harm that they do not perceive. Even the trials and calamities in their lives are for their spiritual growth, as was mentioned earlier.

This verse emphasises the meanings of the previous verse and further encourages those who fear Allāh to do as much as they can to attain His pleasure and to do as much as they can to avoid His displeasure. Since He is aware of all human deeds and their intentions, every opportunity to speak about good and to do righteous deeds should be seized. No good deed should be considered useless as the Prophet (ﷺ) was reported to have said,

اتَّقُوا النَّارَ وَلَوْ بِشِقِّ تَمْرَةٍ

> *"Shield yourselves from the Fire, even if it is only with half of a date."*[161]

Based on the linguistic structure of this verse, it could also be interpreted and translated as:
"Should He not know what He created?"[162]

This is a logical challenge to those who reject religion. Allāh revealed a prescribed system of laws as a guide to life in this world called the *Sharī'ah*. Linguistically speaking, *Sharī'ah* means a path to a water source. It is, so to speak, a map for making it safely through this life to the destination of Paradise.

---

[161] *Sahih Al-Bukhari*, vol. 2, pp. 282-3, no. 494; *Sahih Muslim*, vol. 2, pp. 486-7, nos. 2215-8.

[162] *Tafsīr al-Qur'ān al-'Aẓim*, vol. 4, p. 424.

Without that guide, one resembles a soldier trying to navigate his way through a minefield without a map. That Allāh knows best, is stressed throughout the Qur'ān. For example, He said in *Sūrah al-Baqarah*: **"You may dislike something good for you and like something bad for you."** (2:216)

A lingering doubt which is commonly raised is: "Life keeps changing, but the *Sharī'ah* is unchanging, so it couldn't possibly be appropriate for an era of satellite communication, space travel, etc." On one occasion, Al-Zindānī responded to this by asking the questioner, "Do you see by a different kind of eye than people 1400 years ago?" The answer, of course, was no. "Is your stomach different than the stomach of a person 1400 years ago?" "Are emotions like love and hate different now than for people of the past?" Human nature is, in fact, constant and that is what the *Sharī'ah* addresses.

It should also be noted that the Islamic legal system is fixed in certain areas and open to change in other areas. It is detailed and unchanging in the area of beliefs and worship and in the laws about the unchanging aspects of human nature. For example, sex roles are squarely in this category. Gender feminism[163] is, in reality, a denial of biology. The three key events of any organism's existence are birth, reproduction and death. Human babies are unlike every other animal in the length of time it takes for a human child to be able to take care of itself. Therefore, Allāh prescribed the family as a means of caring for children. Women are biologically designed to bear children and nurture them. Therefore, from the Islamic point of view, it is the responsibility of men to earn a livelihood to support their wives in this critical job. This biological reality is given consideration in the mutual rights and responsibilities of husbands and wives and in the division of inheritance.

---

[163] The belief in the social, economic, and political equality of the sexes. See *Encyclopaedia Britannica*.

Biological reality is also given consideration in the issue of child custody after divorce. According to Islamic law, the child goes to the mother when it is below the age of seven. If she remarries, it passes from her to her mother. [Males tend to be, at best, uninterested in raising the children of another male. Sociobiologists observe that male animals frequently kill the offspring of females they mate with if they know the offspring are not their own.] After the child reaches seven, he/she is allowed to choose the parent they prefer to live with.

Another area that reflects consideration of biological realities is the Islamic dress code.

Social realities are manifest in the laws prohibiting drugs and alcohol, and in the fixed punishments (*ḥudūd*) which deter crime. These realities are also the primary reasons for the prohibition of interest (*ribā*), for the consumer of interest is guaranteed profit without work and without risk of his capital. *Ribā* plays a key role in modern injustice on an international scale. The major central banks of Europe and the US are privately owned. They are given the right to create money out of thin air then charge governments, other banks, corporations and individuals interest for it. The American public (as individuals) alone owes a trillion dollars to Visa and the other main credit card companies.

Some sections of the Islamic legal system are almost without detail, such as the laws of government structure. Allāh left it up to people to work out the details because this is an area where changing times do have an impact on the appropriate structure. Other areas like that of traffic laws, building codes, etc. also reflect the fact that Allāh leaves certain areas for the people of each time and era to work out for themselves. Consequently, the basic law governing social interactions (*muʿāmalāt*) and actions done for worldly benefit is that they are all lawful unless specific evidence exists to prohibit them. This is a sign of Allāh's great kindness to His creatures.

Another feature of Islamic law is that it avoids over-legislation. On the other hand, the Federal Register, which is a record of new US government regulations, publishes hundreds of pages of new regulations every year.

VERSE 15

هُوَ ٱلَّذِي جَعَلَ لَكُمُ
ٱلْأَرْضَ ذَلُولًا فَٱمْشُوا۟ فِي مَنَاكِبِهَا وَكُلُوا۟ مِن رِّزْقِهِۦ ۖ وَإِلَيْهِ ٱلنُّشُورُ

It is He who has made the earth manageable for you, so travel in its regions and eat from His food. But [remember that] the Resurrection and return will be to Him.

Allāh reminds humans that it is He who subdued the earth for them and made travel in it possible. Humans have built roads through forests and deserts, over mountains and rivers and under seas based on the intelligence which God has given them and the manageable characteristics which He gave the elements of the earth. He further encourages human beings to travel in the earth and witness the greatness of Allāh's creation as well as the consequence of disobedience.

قُلْ سِيرُوا۟ فِي ٱلْأَرْضِ فَٱنظُرُوا۟ كَيْفَ بَدَأَ ٱلْخَلْقَ ۚ ثُمَّ ٱللَّهُ
يُنشِئُ ٱلنَّشْأَةَ ٱلْءَاخِرَةَ ۚ إِنَّ ٱللَّهَ عَلَىٰ كُلِّ شَيْءٍ قَدِيرٌ ﴿٢٠﴾

"Say: 'Travel in the land and see how He originated creation, then Allāh will bring forth

the creation of the hereafter. Indeed, Allāh is able to do all things.'"
Sūrah al-'Ankabūt (29):20

قُلْ سِيرُواْ فِي ٱلْأَرْضِ ثُمَّ ٱنظُرُواْ كَيْفَ كَانَ عَٰقِبَةُ
ٱلْمُكَذِّبِينَ ﴿١١﴾

"Say: 'Travel in the land and see what the end of those who rejected the truth was.'"
Sūrah al-An'ām (6):11[164]

Allāh then tells humans to eat the food which He provided for them. He refers to the food as 'His food' in order to stress to His creatures that He is the Provider. It is He who provided certain cultivable plants and domesticated animals for human consumption. Allāh then reminds them that there will be a resurrection and judgment, at which time they will have to give an account regarding how His gifts were used.

Consequently, there are responsibilities which accompany these gifts. A portion of the crops must be shared with the less fortunate:

وَهُوَ ٱلَّذِيٓ
أَنشَأَ جَنَّٰتٍ مَّعْرُوشَٰتٍ وَغَيْرَ مَعْرُوشَٰتٍ وَٱلنَّخْلَ وَٱلزَّرْعَ
مُخْتَلِفًا أُكُلُهُۥ وَٱلزَّيْتُونَ وَٱلرُّمَّانَ مُتَشَٰبِهًا وَغَيْرَ
مُتَشَٰبِهٍ ۚ كُلُواْ مِن ثَمَرِهِۦٓ إِذَآ أَثْمَرَ وَءَاتُواْ حَقَّهُۥ يَوْمَ
حَصَادِهِۦ ۖ

[164] See also 3:137; 16:36; 27:69; and 30:42.

"It is He who produces trellised and untrellised gardens, date-palms, and crops of different shape and taste; olives and pomegranates, similar and dissimilar. Eat their fruit when they bear fruit, and pay what is due on the day of its harvest."
Sūrah al-Anʿām (6):141

This amount, known as *ʿushr*, has been ordained because Allāh has destined that some human beings will have less than others. **"Allāh has favoured some of you over others in sustenance."** (16:71) This is in order to develop the noble characteristics of generosity and compassion in humans. However, there should not be excess in giving, such that one's primary family responsibilities suffer, nor should there be deception nor wastefulness. Allāh states:

وَلَا تُسْرِفُوٓاْ ۚ إِنَّهُۥ لَا يُحِبُّ ٱلْمُسْرِفِينَ ﴿١٤١﴾

"But do not be extravagant. Indeed, He does not like extravagant people."
Sūrah al-Anʿām (6):141

In addition, one is responsible for showing gratitude to Allāh for His provisions and generosity by eating with the etiquette that He has recommended through His Messenger's *Sunnah*. One should say "*Bismillāh*" (In the Name of Allāh) before eating. After eating, one should recite the following supplication:

الْحَمْدُ لِلَّهِ الَّذِي أَطْعَمَنِي هَذَا وَرَزَقَنِيهِ مِنْ غَيْرِ حَوْلٍ مِنِّي وَلَا قُوَّةٍ

Alḥamdu lillāhil ladhī aṭʿamanī hādhā wa razaqanīhi min ghayri ḥawlin minnī wa lā quwwah.

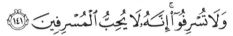

"All praise is for Allāh who fed me this and provided it for me without any might nor power from myself."[165]

[165] *Sunan Abu Dawud*, vol. 3, p. 1125, no. 4012; *Sunan Ibn Majah*, vol. 4, p. 442, no. 3285. Also collected by al-Tirmidhī; authenticated in *'Irwā' Al-Ghalīl*, vol. 7, p. 47.

VERSE 16

ءَأَمِنتُم مَّن فِي ٱلسَّمَآءِ أَن يَخۡسِفَ بِكُمُ ٱلۡأَرۡضَ فَإِذَا هِيَ تَمُورُ ١٦

Do you feel secure that He, Who is over the heaven, will not cause the earth to sink with you? See how it suddenly shakes?

Human beings feel a sense of security on land because Allāh has made it stable most of the time. However, if one rebels against divine guidance, he has no assurance that the earth will not become unstable, as it does in different parts of the world, as a result of his rebellion. In most parts of the earth, people do experience tremors and minor earthquakes as reminders of their vulnerability. The Qur'ān mentions a story of the past in which Qārūn was swallowed up in the midst of his boasting and pride.[166] Prophet Muḥammad (ﷺ) also mentioned that in the future, armies will be sent to attack Muslims seeking refuge at the Ka'bah, but they will be swallowed up by the earth on their route to Makkah.[167] However, Allāh is so merciful to

---

[166] *Sūrah* 28:76-82.

[167] *Sahih Al-Bukhari*, vol. 3, p. 187, no. 329; *Sahih Muslim*, vol. 4, p. 1494-5, nos. 6889-90.

His creatures that He does not hold them to account for all that they do. If He were to do so, they would be completely destroyed as a result. He said: **"If Allāh were to seize humans for their wrongdoing, He would not leave on it [i.e. the earth] a single moving creature."** (16:61)[168]

Allāh describes Himself as *man fis-samā'* (Who is over the heaven).[169] Allāh is not within His creation, but above it. The mystical concepts that Allāh is within every atom of creation or that the human soul is a part of Allāh are both false and of pagan origin. The first concept is known as pantheism in philosophical circles or *waḥdatul-wujūd* in Arabic. It basically makes no distinction between the Creator and His creation. The leading proponent of this belief among Muslims was the 12th century Spanish mystic, Ibn 'Arabī,[170] who described Allāh in his principal works as follows, "Glory be to He, who made all things appear while being their essence."[171] "He is the essence of whatever appears and He is the essence of what is hidden while He appears. The one who sees Him is none other than Himself, and no one is hidden from Him because He appears to Himself while being hidden. He is the One called Abū Sa'īd al-Kharāz[172] as well as the name of other visible beings."[173] Using this belief, Ibn 'Arabī justified idolatry, saying, "The

---

[168] Also see 35:45 and 10:11.

[169] The preposition *fī* usually means 'in'; however, it also means 'on' or 'above' in particular contexts, like this one.

[170] Muhammad ibn 'Alī ibn 'Arabī (1165-1240CE) claimed to possess inner light and knowledge of Allāh's greatest name. He referred to himself as the seal of the sainthood, which he implied was of a higher status than the prophethood. In the centuries following his death, his followers elevated him to the status of saint, and gave him the title of *al-Shaykh al-Akbar* (The Greatest Master), but the majority of Muslim legal scholars considered him a heretic. His principle works are *al-Futūḥāt al-Makkiyyah* and *Fuṣūṣ al-Ḥikam*. (*Shorter Encyclopedia of Islam*, pp. 146-7.)

[171] *Al-Futūḥāt al-Makkiyyah*, vol. 2, p. 604.

[172] Abū Sa'īd Aḥmad ibn 'Īsā (d.893) was the first Muslim mystic to have spoken about the principle of *Fanā* (dissolving the human soul in God).

[173] *Fuṣūṣ al-Ḥikam*, vol. 1, p. 77.

one whose knowledge is perfected (*al-ʿĀrif al-Mukammal*) is one who sees every object of worship as a manifestation of the Divine Reality being worshipped in it. Because of that people call them god though they are stones, trees, animals, humans, planets or angels."[174]

The second concept is known as *ḥulūl* whereby, man becomes a vessel for God's existence or *ittiḥād* whereby the human soul fuses with the world soul. Abū Yazīd al-Bisṭāmī, a 15th century mystic was quoted on one occasion as saying, "I came out of Allāh into Allāh until He cried out from within me saying; 'O you who I am.'"[175] And on another occasion, he was reported to have said, "Praise be to me. I am the Divine Reality. I am the true God. Praise be to me. I must be celebrated by divine praise."[176] Al-Ḥallāj, one of the popular so-called 'saints' in the hierarchy of Muslim 'saints', is famous for his statement *Anal-Ḥaqq* (I am the creative truth), for which he was executed. In defence of that claim, he wrote the following, "If you do not recognise God, at least recognise His sign, I am the creative truth, because through the truth, I am eternal truth. My friends and teachers are Iblīs and Pharaoh. Iblīs was threatened with Hellfire, yet he refused to recant. Pharaoh was drowned in the sea, yet he did not recant, for he would not acknowledge anything between him and God.[177] And I, though I am killed and crucified, and though my hands and feet are cut off, I do not recant."[178]

On the other hand, in the Qur'ān, the angels are referred to as ascending up to God:

---

[174] *Fuṣūṣ al-Ḥikam*, vol. 1, p. 195.

[175] *Tadhkirah al-Awliyā'*, vol. 1, p. 160.

[176] Ibid.

[177] That is, Ḥallāj believed that Iblīs' refusal to prostrate to Adam and Pharaoh's statement **"I am your Lord Most High,"** were both correct.

[178] From *Kitāb al-Ṭawāsīn*, quoted in *Idea of Personality*, p. 32.

تَعْرُجُ ٱلْمَلَٰٓئِكَةُ وَٱلرُّوحُ إِلَيْهِ فِى يَوْمٍ كَانَ مِقْدَارُهُۥ خَمْسِينَ أَلْفَ سَنَةٍ ﴿٤﴾

"The angels and the Spirit (Gabriel) go up to Him in a day whose measure is fifty thousand years."
Sūrah al-Maʿārij (70):4

Prophet Jesus was saved from execution and raised up to God:

إِنِّى مُتَوَفِّيكَ وَرَافِعُكَ إِلَىَّ

"Indeed, I put you to sleep and will take you up to me,"
Sūrah Āl-ʿImrān (3):55

In addition, the Prophet (ﷺ) was reported to have said,

فإذا سألتم الله فسلوه الفردوس ، فإنه أوسط الجنة وفوقه عرش الرحمن

"If you ask Allāh for Paradise, ask for al-Firdaws, for it is the highest part, above which is only the throne of the Most Gracious."[179]

And Allāh stated in the Qur'ān: **"The Most Gracious is above His throne,"** (20:5). Anas ibn Mālik reported that Zaynab bint Jaḥsh used to boast to the other wives of the Prophet (ﷺ) saying, "*You were given in marriage to the Prophet (ﷺ) by your families, while I was married to the Prophet (ﷺ) by Allāh, from above the seven heavens.*"[180]

179 *Sahih Al-Bukhari*, vol. 9, p. 383, no. 519.

180 Ibid., vol. 9, pp. 381-2, nos. 516 & 517.

There is also an authentic narration from Muʿāwiyah ibn al-Ḥakam in which the Prophet (ﷺ) confirms that Allāh is above the heavens. Muʿāwiyah said that he once had a young slave-girl who tended his sheep and he discovered that she had allowed some of them to be lost so he slapped her on her face. On doing so, he immediately realised that he had sinned, for the Prophet (ﷺ) had forbidden striking any person or animal in the face. So he went to the Prophet (ﷺ) and asked whether or not he could free her as a means of atonement. The Prophet (ﷺ) told him to bring the girl. When she came, the Prophet (ﷺ) asked her where Allāh was and she replied, "Above the heavens." He then asked her who he was, and she replied, "You are the Messenger of Allāh." So he turned to Muʿāwiyah and said,

أَعْتِقْهَا فَإِنَّهَا مُؤْمِنَةٌ

"Free her, for she is indeed a believer."[181]

[181] *Sahih Muslim*, vol.1, pp. 271-2, no. 1094; and *Sunan Abu Dawud*, vol. 1, pp. 236-7, no. 930.

VERSE 17

أَمْ أَمِنتُم مَّن فِي ٱلسَّمَآءِ أَن يُرْسِلَ عَلَيْكُمْ حَاصِبًا ۖ فَسَتَعْلَمُونَ كَيْفَ نَذِيرِ ﴿١٧﴾

Or do you feel secure that He, who is over the heaven, will not send a violent whirlwind against you. Soon you will know the result of My Warning?

The disbelievers are further advised to reflect on other natural phenomenon which could become a source of their destruction. Cool breezes in the morning and evening in many places around the world quickly evolve into violent hurricanes, typhoons and tornadoes. Regarding wind, Prophet Muḥammad (ﷺ) was reported to have said,

الرِّيحُ مِنْ رَوْحِ اللهِ، قال سلمة: فَرَوْحُ اللهِ تَأْتِي بِالرَّحْمَةِ وَتَأْتِي بِالْعَذَابِ، فَإِذَا رَأَيْتُمُوهَا فَلَا تَسُبُّوهَا وَسَلُوا اللهَ خَيْرَهَا وَاسْتَعِيذُوا بِاللهِ مِنْ شَرِّهَا

"The wind is from the breath of Allāh; it brings mercy and it brings punishment. So when you

feel it, do not curse it. Instead, ask Allāh for the good in it and ask Allāh's protection from the evil in it."[182]

When the wind would blow, he used to say the following prayer,

اللهم إني أسألك خيرها، وخير ما فيها، وخير ما أرسلت به. وأعوذ بك من شرها، وشر ما فيها، وشر ما أرسلت به

"Allāhumma innī as'aluka khayrahā, wa khayra mā fīhā, wa khayra mā ursilat bih. wa a'ūdhu bika min sharrihā wa sharri mā fīhā, wa sharri mā ursilat bih.

O Allāh. I ask you for its good; the good in it and the good for which it was sent. And I seek Your protection from its evil; the evil in it and the evil for which it was sent."[183]

Allāh threatens the disbelievers, telling them that they will soon know the result of His warnings. It may not come as a natural disaster in this life due to the presence of other good people in their midst. But this life is short, so they will know the severity of Allāh's punishment soon enough.

---

[182] *Sunan Ibn Majah*, vol. 5, pp. 149-50, no. 3727, and *Sunan Abu Dawud*, vol. 3, pp. 1413-4, no. 5078. Aḥmad reported it as *ḥasan*. Al-Albānī authenticated it in *Ṣaḥīḥ al-Kalim al-Ṭayyib*, no.126.

[183] *Sahih Muslim*, vol. 2, p. 425, no. 1962.

VERSE 18

وَلَقَدۡ كَذَّبَ ٱلَّذِينَ مِن قَبۡلِهِمۡ فَكَيۡفَ كَانَ نَكِيرِ ۝١٨

Indeed those before them denied [the truth]. How severe was My disapproval?

Throughout history, those who rejected the Messengers of Allāh were ultimately annihilated. For example, the people in the cities to whom Prophet Lot was sent rejected the divine teachings and were completely destroyed by fierce winds.[184] In fact, most of the great pagan civilisations of the past were devastated by natural disasters at different points in their histories. These events are preserved in narrated folklore as well as in the written histories of many ancient civilisations. Modern archaeological research has uncovered much evidence confirming such events among the Mayans of Central America, the Romans and Greeks in Europe, African civilisations, Persians, Indians and Chinese. Indian civilisations, such as the Aztecs and Incas, were known to have had many gods, including the various forces of nature, which they worshipped

[184] See 17:68 and 29:40.

and offered human sacrifices to. Their large empires were ultimately destroyed and their civilisations came to an end altogether.[185] Unfortunately, these events are individually studied in universities and schools around the world with little or no spiritual impact on those who study them.

---

[185] *Encylopaedia Britannica*, 15th ed., vol. 1, pp.758-9.

VERSE 19

أَوَلَمْ يَرَوْا۟ إِلَى ٱلطَّيْرِ فَوْقَهُمْ صَٰٓفَّٰتٍ وَيَقْبِضْنَ ۚ مَا يُمْسِكُهُنَّ إِلَّا
ٱلرَّحْمَٰنُ ۚ إِنَّهُۥ بِكُلِّ شَىْءٍۭ بَصِيرٌ ﴿١٩﴾

Do they not see the birds above them, spreading out their wings and folding them in? None keeps them up except the Most Gracious. Indeed, He sees everything.

Allāh invites the disbelievers to observe the graceful motion of flying birds in order to reflect on His power. They are asked to reflect on how birds, which are heavier than air, fly. When birds fold their wings, they do not fall from the sky as a plane without wings would. Instead they soar and dive effortlessly using air currents and their aerodynamic design. It was from the observation of the flight of birds and a careful study of their wing design that humans were able to make the first flying machines. Even the latest commercial and military jet airplanes like the Concorde and the F-16 are very bird-like in their overall design. Were people of the past to be told that humans would fly tons of metal into the air, and travel in them from continent to continent, they would have scoffed at the idea. However, humans have learned the principles of flight from the birds and now they do just that. The disbelievers should ponder over who set the laws which keep the birds and the jumbo jets in the air. Humans discovered the laws of flight and learned how to exploit them, but they did not create the laws. Allāh created the laws and He is in control of everything. Humankind should not fool itself. For, no matter how great their technological advances become, their knowledge remains infinitesimally small. As Allāh said, **"The knowledge you were given is very little."**(17:85) Today, humans hurl rockets out of the earth's atmosphere which travel through space to nearby planets. This newly found power should have led them to humility, but it has only increased their arrogance and pride. Instead of turning to Allāh who has already given them the answers, they spend millions annually trying to contact aliens from other galaxies in the hope of finding the answers there. They also spend tens of millions trying to find life on the moon, on Mars, or the moons of other planets in order to justify their unsubstantiated assumption that life developed on earth by accident.

Regarding the birds, it should also be noted that their daily lives are completely in the hands of Allāh. ʿUmar quoted the Prophet (ﷺ) as saying,

لَوْ إِنَّكُمْ تَتَوَكَّلُونَ عَلَى اللهِ حَقَّ تَوَكُّلِهِ لَرَزَقَكُمْ كَمَا يَرْزُقُ الطَّيْرَ ، تَغْدُو خِمَاصاً وَتَرُوحُ بِطَاناً

"If you trusted in Allāh the way He should be trusted, He would provide for you the way He provides for the birds. They leave their nests in the morning with empty stomachs and return at dusk full."[186]

[186] Collected by al-Tirmidhī, Ibn Mājah and Aḥmad (*Al-Hadis*, vol. 1, p. 445, no. 165) and authenticated in *Ṣaḥīḥ al-Jāmiʿ al-Ṣaghīr*, vol. 5-6, p. 60, no. 5130.

Allāh closes this verse with the reminder that He sees everything. Realising and internalising this fact can help a person to rid himself of heedlessness in his actions and cause him to do righteous deeds. When a person is consciously aware of the fact that Allāh is constantly watching him, and that nothing he does can escape His sight, then he will act in a way which pleases Allāh. Once Jibrīl came to the Prophet (ﷺ) and his companions in the form of a man and asked the Prophet (ﷺ) various questions about the religion. At one point, Jibrīl asked the Prophet (ﷺ),

ما الإِحسانُ؟ قال: أَنْ تَعْبُدَ اللهَ كَأَنَّكَ تَراهُ، فَإِنْ لَمْ تَكُنْ تَراهُ فَإِنَّهُ يَراكَ

"What is iḥsān?[187] He (ﷺ) replied, "It is to worship Allāh as though you are seeing him, and though you do not see Him, [know that] He certainly sees you."[188]

---

[187] *Iḥsān*: goodness, the highest level of deeds and worship, perfection.

[188] *Sahih Muslim*, vol. 1, pp. 1-3, no.1.

VERSE 20

أَمَّنْ هَٰذَا ٱلَّذِى هُوَ جُندٌ لَّكُمْ يَنصُرُكُم مِّن دُونِ ٱلرَّحْمَٰنِ ۚ إِنِ ٱلْكَٰفِرُونَ إِلَّا فِى غُرُورٍ

Who besides the Most Gracious can be a supporting army for you? Surely, the disbelievers are in nothing but delusion.

Humans tend to judge power and authority according to the size of a nation's army. However, not even the greatest army which humans could muster, will be of any help against Allāh's punishment. As the corrupt are led off into the Hellfire, they are sarcastically asked about those whom they thought would have been of help to them.

وَيَوْمَ يُنَادِيهِمْ فَيَقُولُ أَيْنَ شُرَكَآءِىَ ٱلَّذِينَ كُنتُمْ تَزْعُمُونَ ﴿٦٢﴾

"Then on the Day of Resurrection, He will call them and say: 'Where are My partners whom you used to argue about?'"
Sūrah al-Qaṣaṣ (28):62

Instead, all the false partners attributed to Allāh will be gathered together in an army as witnesses against the disbelievers.

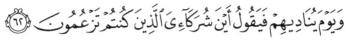

وَاتَّخَذُوا مِن دُونِ اللَّهِ آلِهَةً لَّعَلَّهُمْ يُنصَرُونَ ﴿٧٤﴾
لَا يَسْتَطِيعُونَ نَصْرَهُمْ وَهُمْ لَهُمْ جُندٌ مُّحْضَرُونَ ﴿٧٥﴾

"They have taken gods besides Allāh hoping for their help. But they cannot help them. Instead, they will be brought forward as an army against those who worshipped them."
Sūrah Yā Sīn (36):74-5

The immense variety of false beliefs held by the disbelievers are all satanic delusions, despite the fact that Allāh has clearly warned humans to safeguard themselves from Satan's deception. He said:

إِنَّ وَعْدَ اللَّهِ حَقٌّ ۖ فَلَا تَغُرَّنَّكُمُ الْحَيَاةُ الدُّنْيَا
وَلَا يَغُرَّنَّكُم بِاللَّهِ الْغَرُورُ ﴿٣٣﴾

"Indeed, the Promise of Allāh is true, so do not let the present life (of this world) deceive you, nor let the chief deceiver (i.e. Satan) deceive you about Allāh."
Sūrah Luqmān (31):33

However, they will come to regret their heedlessness in this regard on the Last Day.

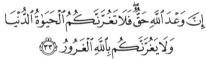

وَقَالَ ٱلشَّيْطَٰنُ
لَمَّا قُضِيَ ٱلْأَمْرُ إِنَّ ٱللَّهَ وَعَدَكُمْ وَعْدَ ٱلْحَقِّ وَوَعَدتُّكُمْ
فَأَخْلَفْتُكُمْ ۖ وَمَا كَانَ لِيَ عَلَيْكُم مِّن سُلْطَٰنٍ إِلَّآ أَن دَعَوْتُكُمْ
فَٱسْتَجَبْتُمْ لِي ۖ فَلَا تَلُومُونِي وَلُومُوٓا۟ أَنفُسَكُم ۖ مَّآ أَنَا۠
بِمُصْرِخِكُمْ وَمَآ أَنتُم بِمُصْرِخِيَّ ۖ إِنِّي كَفَرْتُ بِمَآ
أَشْرَكْتُمُونِ مِن قَبْلُ ۗ إِنَّ ٱلظَّٰلِمِينَ لَهُمْ عَذَابٌ أَلِيمٌ

"When the matter is decided, Satan will say: 'Indeed, Allāh's promise was truthful. I promised you also, but I betrayed you. I had no authority over you. I only invited you and you responded. So do not blame me, but blame yourselves. I cannot help you, nor can you help me. Furthermore, I deny your previous association of me as a partner with Allāh.' Surely the corrupt will have a painful punishment."

Sūrah Ibrāhīm (14):22

Throughout history, Allāh has protected human society from self-destruction by turning its armies against each other. For example, Napoleon's armies were eventually defeated by those of Britain, while Hitler's forces were beaten by the armies of the 'Allied Forces'.

وَلَوْلَا دَفْعُ ٱللَّهِ ٱلنَّاسَ بَعْضَهُم بِبَعْضٍ لَّفَسَدَتِ
ٱلْأَرْضُ وَلَٰكِنَّ ٱللَّهَ ذُو فَضْلٍ عَلَى
ٱلْعَٰلَمِينَ ﴿٢٥١﴾

"If Allāh did not check one set of people with another, the earth would have been filled with

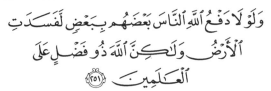

corruption. But Allāh has favoured the worlds with His grace."
Sūrah al-Baqarah (2):251

Humans tend to see the victories as their own, but Allāh's will can be found in all the deciding battles. For example, during World War Two, Hitler's army was defeated by the Russian winter more so than by the Russian army. Had Hitler succeeded in conquering Russia and bringing the Russian forces and resources under his command, the world would have been faced with almost certain defeat. Hitler's loss in Russia was crucial to his ultimate defeat. It was a major turning point in the war. Similarly, in the last major battle of the pagans against Prophet Muḥammad (ﷺ) and the Muslims of Madīnah,[189] it was the 'forces of nature' and not the Muslim army which ultimately defeated the pagan armies. In the night before the final attack, strong winds came and whipped up a dust storm which swept through the enemy encampment, blowing away their tents, putting out their fires and driving off their horses and camels. Consequently, the pagans were forced to break off their attack and return to their provinces in disarray.

[189] This battle was called the "Battle of the Trench" or the "Battle of the Clans".

VERSE 21

أَمَّنْ هَٰذَا ٱلَّذِى يَرْزُقُكُمْ إِنْ أَمْسَكَ رِزْقَهُۥ ۚ بَل لَّجُّوا۟ فِى عُتُوٍّ وَنُفُورٍ ﴿٢١﴾

Who can provide for you if He should withhold His sustenance? None; but they remain stubbornly proud, fleeing [from the truth].

The disbelievers are also asked to reflect on their role in obtaining sustenance. If the clouds do not rain and the wells and rivers run dry, can farmers grow their crops? All of the various means of obtaining food, clothing and shelter depend on the 'forces of nature' which are beyond human control. Modern technology, which enables farmers to cause rain by seeding clouds, can only work if there are clouds already present. Damming rivers and redirecting the flow of their waters to irrigate dry lands depends on melting ice caps or springs to produce the rivers. This reality no one can deny. However, those who have turned away from religion are driven by arrogance and refuse to act on their knowledge. Consequently, Allāh says the following about them:

وَجَحَدُوا۟ بِهَا وَٱسْتَيْقَنَتْهَآ أَنفُسُهُمْ ظُلْمًا وَعُلُوًّا ۚ

"They arrogantly and oppressively denied [Allāh's signs], though their souls were convinced of them."
Sūrah al-Naml (27:14)

Because Allāh is the Provider and Sustainer, humans should not view their material provisions as a sole result of their own efforts. They should recognise that it is actually Allāh who is causing them to obtain everything they have and, in turn, they should thank Him and seek His pleasure alone. This is not an excuse for laziness, nor for people to stop actively searching and working for sustenance, with the belief that Allāh will provide. One must first exert his utmost effort and then place his trust in Allāh. However, considering the fact that everybody's provisions are in Allāh's hands, it does not make sense for a Muslim to disobey Allāh in order to find or keep a job. Such disobedience reflects disbelief in the fact that Allāh is the Provider and belief that the workplace authorities are the true providers. For example, it is a common practice for some Muslim women in the west to take off their *ḥijāb*[190] in order to attain or maintain a job, while with more effort, they can either find another job which does not force them to compromise their practice, or they can obtain their right to religious freedom through the law. Hence, if Allāh wills, He could withhold His provisions from the person, even if he or she did everything to please their boss. Such people neglect Allāh's promise:

وَمَن يَتَّقِ ٱللَّهَ يَجْعَل لَّهُۥ مَخْرَجًا ﴿٢﴾ وَيَرْزُقْهُ مِنْ حَيْثُ لَا يَحْتَسِبُ ۚ

[190] A Muslim woman's required dress code, which includes an outer garment and a headscarf. Some scholars hold that though covering one's face and hands is recommended, it is not compulsory. However, other scholars hold that covering the face and hands is obligatory.

"Whoever fears Allāh, then Allāh will make an outlet for him [from every difficulty] and will provide for him from sources he never imagined."
Sūrah al-Ṭalāq (65):2-3

One must strongly believe the fact that his or her sustenance has already been decreed, and displeasing Allāh to please others will in no way change divine decree. The Prophet (ﷺ) said,

إنَّ أحدَكم يُجمعُ خلقُه في بطنِ أُمِّه أربعينَ يوماً ، ثمَّ يكونُ علقةً مثلَ ذلك ، ثمَّ يكونُ مُضْغةً مثلَ ذلك ثمَّ يبعثُ اللهُ ملَكاً يؤمَرُ بأربعِ كلماتٍ ويقالُ له : اكتبْ عملَه ورزقَه وشقيٌّ أو سعيدٌ . ثمَّ ينفخُ فيه الرُّوحُ

"Indeed the creation of each one of you is brought together in his mother's womb for forty days. Then he is a clot of blood for a like period, then a morsel of flesh for a like period. Then the angel who blows the breath of life into him is sent, and is commanded to [write] four things: his means of livelihood, his life-span, his actions, and whether he will be happy or miserable [in Hereafter]..."[191]

[191] *Sahih Al-Bukhari*, vol. 8, p. 387, no. 593.

VERSE 22

أَفَمَن يَمْشِي مُكِبًّا عَلَىٰ وَجْهِهِۦٓ أَهْدَىٰٓ أَمَّن يَمْشِي سَوِيًّا
عَلَىٰ صِرَٰطٍ مُّسْتَقِيمٍ ﴿٢٢﴾

Is one who walks facing the ground more rightly guided than one who walks facing ahead on a straight path?

A metaphor is used in this verse to highlight the difference between the disbelievers and the believers. The disbeliever is like a person who walks facing the ground. Such a person will surely be totally lost. The disbelievers are unaware of the direction in which they are travelling and they constantly bump into obstacles on the way. Disbelievers are generally ignorant of the true purpose of life. Consequently, the secular societies which they have created are drowning in crime, drugs, immorality and disease. On the other hand, the believer knows the purpose of life and follows the straight path outlined by the prophets of God. Thus, the believer is like one who walks facing ahead on a straight path.

Because the disbelievers choose to walk facing the ground in this life; in the next life Allāh will make them walk on their faces as a means of disgracing them. Allāh says:

ٱلَّذِينَ يُحْشَرُونَ عَلَىٰ وُجُوهِهِمْ إِلَىٰ جَهَنَّمَ أُوْلَٰٓئِكَ شَرٌّ مَّكَانًا وَأَضَلُّ سَبِيلًا ۝٣٤

"Those who will be herded towards hell on their faces will be in the worst of states and the most lost from the path."
Sūrah al-Furqān (25):34

In this regard, Anas ibn Mālik reported that a man asked, "O Prophet of Allāh! Will Allāh gather the disbelievers on their faces on the Day of Resurrection?" He replied,

أَلَيسَ الَّذِي أَمشَاهُ عَلَى الرِّجلَينِ فِي الدُّنيَا قَادِراً عَلَى أَن يُمشِيَهُ عَلَى وَجهِهِ يَومَ القِيَامَة

"Is the One who made him walk on his feet in this world not able to make him walk on his face on the Day of Resurrection?"[192]

[192] *Sahih Al-Bukhari*, vol. 6, p. 269, no. 283.

VERSE 23

قُلْ هُوَ الَّذِي أَنشَأَكُمْ وَجَعَلَ لَكُمُ السَّمْعَ وَالْأَبْصَارَ وَالْأَفْئِدَةَ
قَلِيلًا مَّا تَشْكُرُونَ ﴿٢٣﴾

Say: He is the one who created you, and gave you hearing, sight and hearts. But you rarely give thanks.

Human beings were granted the senses of hearing and sight to gather information, as well as intelligence and perception,[193] with which to process the information and judge its moral implications. Animals, on the other hand, blindly follow their natural instincts and environmental conditioning. Humans should thank Allāh for these favours by using their faculties in accordance with the divinely revealed laws. Consequently, Allāh refers to those who reject His instructions as being worse than the animals. In *Sūrah al-Aʿrāf*, Allāh said:

193 Ibn Kathīr mentioned that hearts referred to perception (*Tafsīr al-Qur'ān al-ʿAẓīm*, vol. 4, p. 426).

وَلَقَدْ ذَرَأْنَا لِجَهَنَّمَ كَثِيرًا مِّنَ الْجِنِّ وَالْإِنسِ ۖ لَهُمْ قُلُوبٌ
لَّا يَفْقَهُونَ بِهَا وَلَهُمْ أَعْيُنٌ لَّا يُبْصِرُونَ بِهَا وَلَهُمْ آذَانٌ لَّا يَسْمَعُونَ
بِهَا ۚ أُولَٰئِكَ كَالْأَنْعَامِ بَلْ هُمْ أَضَلُّ ۚ أُولَٰئِكَ هُمُ الْغَافِلُونَ ﴿١٧٩﴾

"Surely, I have created many of the jinn and humankind for Hell. For, they have hearts, yet they do not understand; they have eyes, yet they do not see; and they have ears, yet they do not hear. They are like cattle. Indeed, they are even more astray."

Sūrah al-Aʿrāf (7):179

Wherever hearing and sight are mentioned as gifts from God, hearing is mentioned first.[194] This could indicate that hearing is even more important than seeing. In fact, the learning capabilities are more dependent on normal hearing than anything else. A child born deaf will have great difficulty in learning language and other things. A child born blind is handicapped, but it is much easier to teach him language and other capabilities. More importantly, however, is the fact that the sense of hearing develops in the human embryo before the sense of sight. The foetus can hear sounds after the 24th week. Subsequently, the sense of sight is developed and by the 28th week, the retina becomes sensitive to light.[195]

---

[194] 16:78; 23:78; 76:2; etc.

[195] *Qur'an & Modern Science*, p. 62.

VERSE 24

قُلْ هُوَ ٱلَّذِى ذَرَأَكُمْ فِى ٱلْأَرْضِ وَإِلَيْهِ تُحْشَرُونَ ﴿٢٤﴾

Say: "He is the one who scattered you in the earth, and you will be gathered before Him."

Prophet Muḥammad (ﷺ) and the believers are instructed in this verse to remind humankind that it was Allāh who created them from a single set of parents, multiplied their numbers, languages and characteristics, and scattered them all over the earth. Had He wished to do so, He could have kept them as a single nation. He says in the Qur'ān:

وَلَوْ شَآءَ ٱللَّهُ لَجَعَلَكُمْ أُمَّةً وَٰحِدَةً

"If Allāh wished, He could have made you one nation."
Sūrah al-Mā'idah (5):48

The purpose for the diversity among humans is for them to become familiar with each other. The variation of nations and tribes, clans and families encourages human curiosity in a way that uniformity does not. Allāh states in *Sūrah al-Ḥujurāt*:

يَٰٓأَيُّهَا ٱلنَّاسُ إِنَّا خَلَقۡنَٰكُم مِّن ذَكَرٖ وَأُنثَىٰ وَجَعَلۡنَٰكُمۡ شُعُوبٗا وَقَبَآئِلَ لِتَعَارَفُوٓاْۚ إِنَّ أَكۡرَمَكُمۡ عِندَ ٱللَّهِ أَتۡقَىٰكُمۡۚ إِنَّ ٱللَّهَ عَلِيمٌ خَبِيرٞ ﴿١٣﴾

"O humankind, indeed I have created you from a male and female, and made you into peoples and tribes to know each other."
Sūrah al-Ḥujurāt (49):13

Knowledge of each other also includes awareness of family ties, which define the boundaries of marriage and incest, and delineate family obligations and financial responsibilities through the inheritance laws. Consequently, Islām places great emphasis on the clear identification of family relationships. The Prophet (ﷺ) himself said,

تَعَلَّمُوا مِنْ أَنْسَابِكُمْ مَا تَصِلُونَ بِهِ أَرْحَامَكُمْ

"Learn enough about your lineages to know your blood relatives and treat them accordingly."[196]

Although it is the duty of the Islamic state to take care of its citizens, the primary responsibility falls first on family members. Therefore, according to Islamic law, blood relationships should be clearly defined, and any tampering with them is strictly forbidden. Due to the fact that the Arabs used to give their adopted sons their own names, Allāh forbade it. Ibn 'Umar reported that after the Prophet (ﷺ) freed Zayd ibn Ḥārithah and adopted him, people used to address Zayd as "Zayd ibn Muḥammad" until the following verse was revealed:

---

[196] Reported by Abū Hurayrah in *Sunan al-Tirmidhī* and authenticated in *Ṣaḥīḥ Sunan al-Tirmidhī*, vol. 2, pp. 189-90.

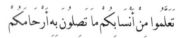

ٱدْعُوهُمْ لِآبَآئِهِمْ هُوَ أَقْسَطُ عِندَ ٱللَّهِ

"Call them by their fathers' names, it is more just in the Sight of Allāh."
Sūrah al-Aḥzāb (33):5[197]

The Prophet (ﷺ) later said,

مَنِ ادَّعَى إِلَى غَيْرِ أَبِيهِ، وَهُوَ يَعْلَمُ أَنَّهُ غَيْرُ أَبِيهِ، فَالْجَنَّةُ عَلَيْهِ حَرَامٌ

"Whoever knowingly attributes his fatherhood to someone other than his real father will be excluded from Paradise."[198]

And on another occasion, he was reported to have said,

أَيُّمَا رَجُلٍ ادَّعَى لِغَيْرِ أَبِيهِ وَهُوَ يَعْلَمُهُ، إِلَّا كَفَرَ

"Whoever deliberately allows himself to be called the son of someone other than his father is guilty of disbelief."[199]

Consequently, at the time of marriage, a woman is not supposed to take the husband's family name. This amounts to denying her own genealogy. Instead, she retains her own family name. Likewise, when someone converts or reverts to Islām, his or her family name should not be changed. A person may change only his or her given first name.[200]

---

[197] *Sahih Al-Bukhari*, vol. 6, p. 290, no. 305; *Sahih Muslim*, vol. 1, p. 42, no. 120; and *Sunan Abu Dawud*, vol. 3, pp. 1417-8, no. 5095.

[198] *Sahih Al-Bukhari*, vol. 8, p. 500, no. 758; *Sahih Muslim*, vol. 1, p. 42, no.120; and *Sunan Abu Dawud*, vol. 3, p. 1417, no. 5094.

[199] *Sahih Al-Bukhari*, vol. 4, p. 467, no. 711; *Sahih Muslim*, vol. 1, pp. 41-2, no.118; and *Sunan Abu Dawud*, vol. 3, pp. 1417-8, no. 5095.

[200] See *Tafseer Surah al-Hujuraat*, pp. 112-8, for more detail on the Islamic naming system.

Allāh instructs the Prophet (ﷺ) and the believers to stress to the disbelievers that it was Allāh who spread humans throughout the earth in order to remind them that they will be gathered before Him one day. Surely, He who was able to scatter them can gather them. Belief in the Day of Resurrection is one of the six pillars of faith. This belief serves to maintain focus and a sense of purpose in one's life. Knowledge that Allāh will one day question a humans' each and every deed creates careful deliberation in one's actions. In order to produce and enhance this *taqwā* (God-consciousness), Allāh constantly reminds humankind of this distressful day in the Qur'ān, using extremely vivid descriptions. One should reflect upon these and analyse how he or she is spending his or her life. The Prophet (ﷺ) said,

لَا تَزُولُ قَدَمَا ابْنِ آدَمَ يَوْمَ الْقِيَامَةِ مِنْ عِنْدِ رَبِّهِ حَتَّى يُسْأَلَ عَنْ خَمْسٍ: عَنْ عُمْرِهِ فِيمَا أَفْنَاهُ، وَعَنْ شَبَابِهِ فِيمَا أَبْلَاهُ، وَعَنْ مَالِهِ مِنْ أَيْنَ اكْتَسَبَهُ وَفِيمَا أَنْفَقَهُ وَمَاذَا عَمِلَ فِيمَا عَلِمَ

"The feet of [a person] will not move [forward] from near his Lord on the Day of Judgment until he is asked about five things: his life and how he spent it, his youth and what he did with it, his wealth and how he earned and spent it, and about what he acted on from the knowledge he gained."[201]

[201] *Ṣaḥīḥ Sunan al-Tirmidhī*, vol 2, p. 290, no. 1970.

VERSE 25

وَيَقُولُونَ مَتَىٰ هَٰذَا ٱلْوَعْدُ إِن كُنتُمْ صَٰدِقِينَ ﴿٢٥﴾

They ask: "When will this promised event take place?[202] *— if you are telling the truth."*

When informed about being gathered before Allāh, the disbelievers scornfully demand to know the exact date and time that the Resurrection and Judgement will begin. Even if they were informed of the date, they would not believe it, because they already rejected the whole concept of resurrection and judgment. Had they believed in a judgment, they would not have rejected the messengers of God and their messages. Allāh quotes their ridicule of the Hour in *Sūrah al-Jāthiyah*:

وَإِذَا قِيلَ إِنَّ وَعْدَ ٱللَّهِ حَقٌّ وَٱلسَّاعَةُ لَا رَيْبَ فِيهَا قُلْتُم
مَّا نَدْرِى مَا ٱلسَّاعَةُ إِن نَّظُنُّ إِلَّا ظَنًّا وَمَا نَحْنُ بِمُسْتَيْقِنِينَ ﴿٣٢﴾

"And when it is said, 'Indeed, Allāh's promise is true and there is no doubt about the coming

[202] That is, the Day of Resurrection.

of the Hour,' you responded, 'We do not know what the Hour is. We think it is only an opinion and we do not believe in it.'"
Sūrah al-Jāthiyah (45):32

and their mockery of the Resurrection in *Sūrah Qāf*:

أَءِذَا مِتۡنَا وَكُنَّا تُرَابٗاۖ ذَٰلِكَ رَجۡعُۢ بَعِيدٞ ﴿٣﴾

"When we die and become dust [we will be resurrected]? That is a far-fetched return."
Sūrah Qāf (50):3

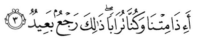

VERSE 26

قُلْ إِنَّمَا ٱلْعِلْمُ عِندَ ٱللَّهِ وَإِنَّمَآ أَنَا۠ نَذِيرٌ مُّبِينٌ ﴿٢٦﴾

Say: "Knowledge of it[203] is with Allāh alone, and I am only an outspoken warner."

Exact knowledge of the Final Hour belongs to Allāh alone. It is stated in many places in the Qur'ān that none besides Allāh has precise knowledge of the time of the Last Day. For example, in *Sūrah al-Aʿrāf*, God says:

يَسْـَٔلُونَكَ عَنِ ٱلسَّاعَةِ
أَيَّانَ مُرْسَىٰهَا ۖ قُلْ إِنَّمَا عِلْمُهَا عِندَ رَبِّى ۖ لَا يُجَلِّيهَا لِوَقْتِهَآ إِلَّا هُوَ ۚ ثَقُلَتْ
فِى ٱلسَّمَـٰوَٰتِ وَٱلْأَرْضِ ۚ لَا تَأْتِيكُمْ إِلَّا بَغْتَةً ۗ يَسْـَٔلُونَكَ كَأَنَّكَ حَفِىٌّ
عَنْهَا ۖ قُلْ إِنَّمَا عِلْمُهَا عِندَ ٱللَّهِ وَلَـٰكِنَّ أَكْثَرَ ٱلنَّاسِ لَا يَعْلَمُونَ ﴿١٨٧﴾

"When they ask you about the Hour with regard to its appointed time, tell them:

[203] Of its exact time.

'Knowledge of it is with my Lord alone. None can reveal its time except He. Its burden is heavy in the heavens and the earth and it will only come upon you suddenly.' When they ask you as if you have good knowledge of it, tell them: 'Knowledge of it is with Allāh alone, but most humans do not realise it."

Sūrah al-Aʿrāf (7):187[204]

ʿAbdullāh narrated that Allāh's Messenger (ﷺ) said, "*The keys of the unseen are five:* ***'Indeed, the knowledge of the Hour is with Allāh alone. He sends down the rain, and knows what is in the wombs.[205] No person knows what he will earn tomorrow, and no person knows which land he will die in. Indeed, Allāh is All-Knowing and All-Aware.'***" (31:34)[206]

ʿUmar ibn al-Khaṭṭāb said,

---

[204] See also: 31:34; 43:85; and 79:42-44.

[205] The fact that ultrasound allows us to see the fetus inside the womb and doctors can even determine the sex of the fetus using amniocentesis and ultrasound does not contradict this verse. In responding to this question, Shaykh ʿAbdul-Majīd al-Zindānī used a principle of *uṣūl al-fiqh* which states that a text which mentions a point without elaboration must be understood in light of texts which elaborate the point and restrict it. A variant narration of this *ḥadīth* quotes Allāh's Messenger as saying, "*The keys of the Unseen are five. No one knows them except Allāh. None knows what will happen tomorrow except Allāh. No one knows what the wombs absorb (taghūth) except Allāh...*" The word *taghūth* has two meanings: 'to decrease' and 'to absorb'. [It is used in the second sense in *Sūrah Hūd* (11):44. After Noah's flood, the earth was made to absorb the standing water.] Al-Bukhārī placed Ibn ʿUmar's narration as a commentary on verse 8 of *Sūrah al-Raʿd* (13): ***"Allāh knows what every woman bears and what the wombs absorb and [by what they] increase."*** Two states of the womb are identified in this verse: the state of absorption and the state of increase. Fertilisation occurs when a sperm cell unites with the woman's egg in the fallopian tube. The fertilised egg reaches the uterus in 4-5 days. It spends a day or two floating freely in the uterine fluids, then it will implant itself in the lining of the uterus. At about ten days after conception, it is fully embedded or 'absorbed' into the layers of the uterine wall. The defect in the uterine surface is plugged by a blood clot and by cellular debris. There is virtually no sign now on the uterine surface that the fertilised egg is buried underneath. After about two days the area begins to show a slight swelling. The womb has now entered the stage of increase. At the implantation stage, a woman is not even aware that she is pregnant because she has not missed her period yet. After forty-some days, an angel is sent to record the child's sex and physical details as well as its life-span, sustenance and whether it will eventually go to heaven or hell. It is obvious that Allāh's knowledge of what is in the womb is no longer exclusive from this point on. It is at this stage that ultrasound and other detection techniques can give us information about the fetus.

[206] *Sahih Al-Bukhari*, vol. 6, pp. 119-20, no. 151.

بينا نحنُ عندَ رسولِ اللهِ ذاتَ يومٍ، إذ طلعَ علينا رجلٌ شديدُ بياضِ الثِّيابِ، شديدُ سوادِ الشعرِ، لا يُرى عليه أثرُ السفرِ، ولا يعرفُه منا أحدٌ، حتى جلسَ إلى النبيِّ. فأسندَ ركبتيهِ إلى ركبتيهِ، ووضعَ كفَّيهِ على فخذيهِ وقال: يا محمدُ! أخبرني عن الإسلامِ؟. فقال رسولُ اللهِ: الإسلامُ أنْ تشهدَ أنْ لا إلهَ إلا اللهُ وأنَّ محمداً رسولُ اللهِ، وتُقيمَ الصلاةَ وتؤتيَ الزكاةَ، وتصومَ رمضانَ، وتحجَّ البيتَ، إنِ استطعتَ إليه سبيلاً قال: صدقتَ. قال فعجبنا له، يسألُه ويصدِّقُه. قال: فأخبرني عن الإيمانِ!. قال: أنْ تؤمنَ باللهِ، وملائكتِه، وكتبِه، ورسلِه، واليومِ الآخرِ، وتؤمنَ بالقدرِ خيرِه وشرِّه. قال: صدقتَ. قال: فأخبرني عن الإحسانِ؟. قال: أنْ تعبدَ اللهَ كأنَّك تراه. فإنْ لم تكنْ تراه، فإنه يراكَ قال: فأخبرني عن الساعةِ؟. قال: ما المسؤولُ عنها بأعلمَ من السائلِ قال: فأخبرني عن أماراتِها. قال: أنْ تلدَ الأمةُ ربَّتها. وأنْ ترى الحفاةَ العراةَ، العالةَ، رعاءَ الشاءِ، يتطاولونَ في البنيانِ. قال ثم انطلقَ. فلبثتُ ملياً. ثم قال لي: يا عمرُ! أتدري من السائلُ؟ قلتُ: اللهُ ورسولُه أعلمُ قال: فإنه جبريلُ. أتاكم يعلِّمكم دينَكم.

"While we were sitting with the Messenger of Allāh (ﷺ) there appeared before us a man whose clothes were exceedingly white and whose hair was jet black. No signs of journeying were to be seen on him, and none of us knew him. He walked up and sat down in front of the Prophet (ﷺ), resting his knees against his and placing the palms of his hands on his thighs. He said: 'O Muḥammad, tell me about Islām.' The Messenger of Allāh (ﷺ) replied: 'Islām is to testify that there is no god worthy of worship but Allāh and Muḥammad is the Messenger of Allāh, to perform the prayers, to pay zakāh,[207] *to fast in Ramaḍān, and to make the pilgrimage to the House*[208] *if you are able to do so.' He said: 'You have spoken rightly.' We were amazed at him asking him and then telling him that he had spoken rightly. He then asked: 'Then tell me about īmān (faith).' The Prophet (ﷺ) replied: 'It is to believe in Allāh, His angels, His books, His messengers, the Last Day, and the good and evil of destiny.' He said: 'You have spoken rightly. He then asked: Tell me about Iḥsān.*[209] *The Prophet (ﷺ) replied: It is to worship Allāh as though you are seeing Him, and though you do not see Him, He sees you.' He asked: 'Then tell me about the Hour.'*[210] *The Prophet (ﷺ) replied: 'The one questioned about it knows no better than the questioner.' He asked: 'Then tell me about [some of] its signs.' The Prophet (ﷺ) replied: 'That the slave-girl will give birth to her*

[207] Often rendered as "alms-tax" or "poor-due", it is a tax levied on a person's wealth and distributed among the poor.

[208] The Ka'bah in Makkah.

[209] The word *iḥsān* means "to master or be proficient at".

[210] i.e.: of the Day of Judgment.

mistress[211] *and that you will see barefoot, naked, destitute herdsmen competing in constructing lofty buildings.' The man then left and I stayed for a while. Then the Prophet (ﷺ) said: "Umar, do you know who the questioner was?' I replied: 'Allāh and His Messenger know best.' He said: 'It was Gabriel, who came to teach you your religion.'"*[212]

It is also recorded in the New Testament, Gospel according to Mark 13:31-2, that Prophet Jesus also denied knowledge of the Hour, saying, "*Heaven and the earth shall pass away but my word shall not pass away, but of that Day or Hour no man knoweth, neither the angels in the heaven nor the Son but the Father.*"

Consequently, for any Muslim to profess this knowledge would be heresy. In 1980, in the United States, Rashad Khalifa[213] alleged that he had discovered this divine secret. He claimed that the 14 sets of Qur'ānic "Initials"[214] were actually

---

[211] This phrase has been interpreted in different ways. Al-Nawawī, in his commentary on *Ṣaḥīḥ Muslim*, explained that it meant slave-girls would give birth to sons and daughters who would become free and so be the masters of those who gave birth to them. The word *amah*, normally translated "slave-girl", also means a woman in that we are all slaves or servants of God. The phrase would then mean: "When a woman will give birth to her master," i.e. a time will come when children will have so little respect for their mothers that they will treat them like servants.
The commentators also point out that here the word *rabbah* (mistress) includes the masculine *rabb* (master). *Sharḥ al-Nawawī 'alā Ṣaḥīḥ Muslim*, vol. 1, p. 194. *Fatḥ al-Bārī*, vol. 1, p. 149.

[212] *Sahih Muslim*, vol. 1, pp. 1-3, no. 1.

[213] Born in Egypt in 1935, he came to the U.S.A. in 1959, where he completed a doctorate in biochemistry in the early 1960s. He later set up a mosque in Tucson, Arizona in 1979, and remained its *Imām* until 1990, when he was assassinated. During the seventies, Dr. Khalifa claimed to have discovered that the number 19 was the basis of the mathematical miracle of the Qur'ān. In the 80s, he later claimed knowledge of the Day of Judgment and denied the authenticity of *ḥadīth*. Following that, he claimed that two verses of the Qur'ān were false because they contradicted his mathematical calculations, and finally, in the late '80s, he claimed prophethood (*Mission to America*, pp. 137-168).

[214] The 14 letters of the alphabet which begin 29 chapters of the Qur'ān. See *The Qur'an's Numerical Miracle*, pp.54-58, for a detailed discussion of their meaning and significance.

14 sets of numbers whose total was 1,709. He further claimed that 1,709 represented the number of years that the Prophet Muhammad's message would last. That is, the end of the world would take place in the year 2201.[215] Actually, Dr. Khalifa borrowed this calculation from a quote in a 15th century C.E. text on Qur'ānic sciences, *Al-Itqān fī 'Ulūm al-Qur'ān.* In it, the author, al-Suyūṭī, quoted a variety of opinions concerning the meaning and significance of the Arabic letters prefixed to the Qur'ānic chapters. Among the more extreme opinions quoted was that of a 12th century grammarian, al-Suhaylī, who said, "Perhaps the number of prefixed letters, when the repetitions are removed, are there to indicate how long this (Muslim) world will last." The author then quoted the total rejection of al-Suhaylī's statement by one of the leading scholars of his day.

In the end of the Arabic edition of his presentation of the 19 theory, Rashad Khalifa actually attempted to attribute numerology and the calculation of the world's end from the Qur'ānic initials to the Prophet Muḥammad (ﷺ) himself! His whole argument was based on what he called "a famous historic event" narrated in the form of a *ḥadīth* in *Tafsīr al-Bayḍāwī.*[216] Concerning the *ḥadīth* and such claims, the 14th century CE classical commentator of the Qur'ān, Ibn Kathīr said the following:[217]

> Those who assume that they [the prefixed Arabic letters] indicate time periods from which the dates of events, calamities and Armageddon may be deduced,

---

[215] On page 221 of his Arabic presentation of the theory, *Mu'jizah al-Qur'an al Karim*, he states the following: "We can clearly see that the end of the world as set by the Qur'an will be—by Allah's will—309 lunar years or 300 solar years after the year of discovery (1980/1400 A.H.)... This means that the year following 1709 A.H. will be the last year of the world, the year 1710 A.H.... and this number is a multiple of 19..."

[216] *Mu'jizah al-Qur'an al-Karim*, pp. 215-7.

[217] *The Qur'an's Numerical Miracle*, pp. 48-9.

have claimed knowledge which they do not have and have speculated where they had no right to speculate. There is however, an inauthentic *ḥadīth* on this subject, which actually confirms the falsity of this line of thought. It is narrated by Muḥammad ibn Isḥāq on the authority of al-Kalbī from Jābir ibn ʿAbdillāh who said, "Once Abū Yāsir ibn Akhṭab passed by the Prophet (ﷺ) as he was reciting the opening words of *Sūrah al-Baqarah*: ***'Alif, Lām, Mīm, this is the book wherein there is no doubt.'*** Then he went to his brother Ḥuyayy who was with some other Jews and said: 'Do you know, by Allāh, that I have heard Muḥammad recite "*Alif, Lām, Mīm* this is the book wherein there is no doubt," among what was revealed to him?' After expressing surprise, Ḥuyayy and these men went to the Prophet (ﷺ) and told him what had been reported to them and asked if Gabriel had brought that message from Allāh. When he said that he had, they said: 'Allāh sent prophets before you, but we do not know of anyone of them being told how long his kingdom would last and how long his community would last.' Ḥuyayy went back to his men and said to them: 'Alif is 1; Lām is 30; and Mīm is 40. That is equal to 71 years. Are you going to adopt a religion whose kingdom and community will last for only 71 years?' Then he went to the Prophet and said, 'Have you anything else, Muḥammad?' He replied 'Yes, *Alif Lām Mīm Ṣād*.' Ḥuyayy said, 'This, by Allāh, is more weighty and longer: Alif is 1: Lām is 30; Mīm is 40, Ṣād is 90. That is equal to 161 years.' Similar questions were asked and answered in respect to *Alif Lām Rā* 231; *Alif Lām Mām Rā* 271. Then he said,

> 'Your situation seems obscure to us, Muḥammad, so that we do not know whether you will have a short or long duration.' When they left him, Abū Yāsir said to his brother Ḥuyayy and the others, 'How do you know that all these totals should not be added together to make a grand total of 734 years?' They answered, 'His affair is obscure to us.'"[218] This *ḥadīth* revolves around Muḥammad ibn al-Sā'ib al-Kalbī whose solitary narrations are considered unreliable."[219]

Although nobody knows the exact time of the Day of Judgment, Allāh has revealed signs of its coming to his messengers. Most of the minor signs have already appeared. The Prophet (ﷺ) pointed out some of these minor signs in the following comprehensive *ḥadīth*: Abū Hurayrah narrated that the Prophet (ﷺ) said,

لَا تَقُومُ السَّاعَةُ حَتَّى تَقْتَتِلَ فِئَتَانِ عَظِيمَتَانِ تَكُونُ بَيْنَهُمَا مَقْتَلَةٌ عَظِيمَةٌ، دَعْوَتُهُمَا
وَاحِدَةٌ، وَحَتَّى يُبْعَثَ دَجَّالُونَ كَذَّابُونَ قَرِيبٌ مِنْ ثَلَاثِينَ كُلُّهُمْ يَزْعُمُ
أَنَّهُ رَسُولُ اللهِ، وَحَتَّى يُقْبَضَ الْعِلْمُ، وَتَكْثُرَ الزَّلَازِلُ، وَيَتَقَارَبَ الزَّمَانُ، وَتَظْهَرَ
الْفِتَنُ، وَيَكْثُرَ الْهَرْجُ وَهُوَ الْقَتْلُ، وَحَتَّى يَكْثُرَ فِيكُمُ الْمَالُ فَيَفِيضَ حَتَّى
يُهِمَّ رَبَّ الْمَالِ مَنْ يَقْبَلُ صَدَقَتَهُ، وَحَتَّى يَعْرِضَهُ فَيَقُولَ الَّذِي يَعْرِضُهُ عَلَيْهِ: لَا أَرَبَ
لِي بِهِ، وَحَتَّى يَتَطَاوَلَ النَّاسُ فِي الْبُنْيَانِ، وَحَتَّى يَمُرَّ الرَّجُلُ بِقَبْرِ الرَّجُلِ
فَيَقُولُ: يَا لَيْتَنِي مَكَانَهُ، وَحَتَّى تَطْلُعَ الشَّمْسُ مِنْ مَغْرِبِهَا

---

[218] For Ibn Isḥāq's narration of the *ḥadīth*, see *The Life of Muhammad*, pp. 256-7.

[219] *Tafsīr al-Qur'ān al-'Aẓīm*, vol. 1, p. 61. In fact, some scholars accused al-Kalbī of lying. *Taqrīb al-Tahdhīb*, p. 479, no. 5901.

"The Hour will not be established until: (1) two big groups fight each other whereupon there will be a great number of casualties on both sides and they will be following one and the same religion; (2) about thirty dajjāls (liars) appear, and each one of them will claim that he is a messenger of Allāh; (3) religious knowledge is taken away; (4) earthquakes increase in number; (5) time will pass quickly; (6) fitnahs (trials and afflictions) will appear; (7) murder will increase; (8) wealth will be in abundance, so much so that a wealthy person will be worried that no one will accept his charity, and whenever he will present it to someone, that person will say, 'I am not in need of it'; (9) the people compete with one another in constructing high buildings; (10) when passing by a grave, a man will say, ' If only I were in his place'; (11) the sun rises from the west..."[220]

The major signs are: the appearance of al-Masīḥ al-Dajjāl (the false messiah), the appearance of the Mahdī, the reappearance of Gog and Magog, the reappearance of Prophet Jesus (peace be with him), the rising of the sun from the west, the beast, and the gathering fire. Details of the first four listed above will be briefly discussed.[221] The false messiah will appear from an area east of Madīnah, based on the Prophet's statement,

إِنَّ الدَّجَّالَ يَخْرُجُ مِنْ أَرْضٍ بِالْمَشْرِقِ يُقَالُ لَهَا خُرَاسَانُ يَتْبَعُهُ أَقْوَامٌ كَأَنَّ وُجُوهَهُمُ الْمِجَانُّ الْمُطْرَقَةُ

"The Dajjāl will appear from a land in the east called Khurasān. He will be accompanied by

---

[220] *Sahih Al-Bukhari*, vol. 9, pp. 180-82, no. 237.

[221] For more details on the major signs of the Day of Judgment, see *But Some of its Signs Have Already Come*, by A. Hijazi (published by *Al-Fustat Magazine*, Arlington, Texas, 1995).

people whose faces are like forged shields."[222]

One of the many *ḥadīths* describing him was narrated by Abū Umāmah, who reported Allāh's Messenger (ﷺ) as saying,

إنه لم تكن فتنة في الأرض، منذ ذرأ الله ذرية آدم، أعظم من فتنة
الدجال... فيقول: أنا ربكم. ولا ترون ربكم حتى تموتوا. وإنه أعور. وإن
ربكم ليس بأعور. وإنه مكتوب بين عينيه: كافر. يقرأه كل مؤمن، كاتب
أو غير كاتب. وإن من فتنته أن معه جنة ونارا. فناره جنة وجنته نار. فمن
ابتلي بناره، فليستغث بالله وليقرأ فواتح الكهف

"O people! There has not been a trial on the face of the earth, since the creation of Adam, greater than the trial of the Dajjāl...He will say, 'I am your lord!' However, you will not see your Lord until after you die. He is blind in one eye. Your Lord is not blind in the eye. The word kāfir (disbeliever) will be written between his eyes. Every believer, whether literate or illiterate, will be able to read it. As a part of his trial, he will have a paradise and a fire. (In reality) his fire is a paradise and his paradise is a fire. Whoever is tested with his fire, let him seek refuge with Allāh and recite the beginning of Sūrah al-Kahf..."[223]

---

[222] Narrated by Abū Bakr; collected by al-Tirmidhī and al-Ḥākim, *al-Mustadrak*, vol. 4, p. 527; authenticated in *Ṣaḥīḥ Sunan al-Tirmidhī*, vol. 2, p. 248, no. 1824.

[223] Collected by Ibn Mājah (*Sunan Ibn Majah*, vol. 5, pp. 382-3, no. 4077), Ibn Khuzaymah, al-Ḥākim, and al-Ḍiyā'; authenticated in *Ṣaḥīḥ al-Jāmiʿ al-Ṣaghīr*, no. 7875. The Prophet (ﷺ) also said, "*Whoever memorises the first ten verses from Sūrah al-Kahf will be protected from the trial of Dajjāl.*" *Sahih Muslim*, vol. 2, p. 386-7, no. 1766.

The Dajjāl will enter every city except for Makkah and Madīnah, which will be guarded by angels.[224] He will stay on earth for forty days. One of these days will be as long as a year, one day will be as long as a month, one day will be as long as a week, and the remainder of the days will be like the ordinary days we experience. He will finally be killed by Prophet Jesus, after Jesus' descent.[225]

The Mahdī will be a pious man having the name of the Prophet (ﷺ), Muḥammad ibn ʿAbdillāh, and following the Prophet's guidance. He will righteously rule the Muslims for seven years and the earth will be filled with justice.[226] Prophet Jesus (ﷺ) will descend before the end of the Mahdī's reign and will pray behind the Mahdī.[227] He will fight the people to accept Islām, banish the *jizyah*,[228] break the cross, and kill the pigs. He will kill the false messiah, as mentioned earlier, and he will remain on earth for forty years.[229] Gog and Magog are a group of people who are held behind a dam, as mentioned in the Qur'ān.[230] They will dig the dam and emerge before the Last Day. They will drink all the water on the earth and will

---

[224] *Sahih Muslim*, vol. 4, p. 1518, no. 7017.

[225] *Sharḥ al-Nawawī ʿalā Ṣaḥīḥ Muslim*, vol. 18, pp. 63-70.

[226] *Sunan Abu Dawud*, vol. 3, p. 1191, no. 4272; authenticated in *Ṣaḥīḥ Sunan Abū Dāwūd*, vol. 3, p. 808, no. 3604.

[227] The Prophet said, *"How will you be when Jesus, the son of Mary, descends among you and your leader is among you?" Sahih Al-Bukhari*, vol. 4, p. 437, no. 658. In another *hadīth* he stated, *"There will always be a portion of my Ummah who will fight for the truth. They will remain prominent until the Day of Judgment. Then Jesus, the son of Mary, will descend and their leader will say to him, 'Lead us in ṣalāh.' But he will say, 'No, for verily some among you are [to be] leaders of the rest. [It is] the honour Allāh has granted to this Ummah.'" Sahih Muslim*, vol. 1, p. 94, no. 293. Most scholars interpret the leader referred to in these *ḥadīths* to be the Mahdī.

[228] Tax taken from Christians and Jews living under Muslim rule. It will be banished because all people will have no choice but to accept Islām or be killed.

[229] *Sunan Abu Dawud*, vol. 3, p. 1203, no. 4310; authenticated in *Ṣaḥīḥ Sunan Abū Dāwūd*, vol. 3, pp. 815-6, no. 3635.

[230] 18:95-7 and 21:96.

overwhelm the people with their massive corruption. Allāh will send worms to attack them until they die.[231]

Allāh ends this verse with a reminder that the Prophet's role was to explain the revelation clearly and warn people of the grave consequences that would result from their rejection of the message. He was not responsible to see to it that their hearts become guided, as this is only in Allāh's hands, but merely to convey the message. In another verse, Allāh reassures His Messenger (ﷺ):

وَّإِن تَوَلَّوْاْ فَإِنَّمَا عَلَيْكَ ٱلْبَلَٰغُ ۗ

"But if they turn away [from divine guidance], then [know that] your only responsibility is to convey [the message]."
Sūrah Āl-ʿImrān (3):20

Similarly, all Muslims are required to submit to the message brought by their beloved Prophet (ﷺ), then to convey it to the people. While calling people to Islām, Muslims should bear a few matters in mind. Firstly, they should follow the methodology and example of the Prophet and his Companions in *daʿwah* (inviting others to Islām). In accord with the Prophet's methodology, Muslims should concentrate on calling people to *tawḥīd* first and the other fundamentals of Islām and *īmān*. They should concern themselves with passing authentic knowledge of the *Sunnah*, rather than calling people to overthrow various governments in order to supposedly establish Allāh's law. The state of the Muslim *Ummah* today is extremely pathetic due to the fact that the Muslim masses have left the teachings of the Qur'ān and authentic Sunnah and have focused all of their interests in attaining the "goods"

[231] Collected by Aḥmad, Ibn Mājah (*Sunan Ibn Majah*, vol. 2, p. 389, nos. 4080) and al-Ḥākim; authenticated in *Ṣaḥīḥ al-Jāmiʿ al-Ṣaghīr*, no. 2276.

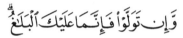

of this deceiving *dunyā* (world). The Prophet (ﷺ) predicted this in various statements. For example, he said,

يُوشَكُ أَنْ تَدَاعَى عَلَيْكُمُ الأُمَمُ مِنْ كُلِّ أُفُقٍ كَمَا تَدَاعَى الأَكَلَةُ عَلَى
قَصْعَتِهَا ، قَالَ : قُلْنَا : يَا رَسُولَ اللهِ ، أَمِنْ قِلَّةٍ بِنَا يَوْمَئِذٍ؟ قَالَ : أَنْتُمْ يَوْمَئِذٍ
كَثِيرٌ وَلَكِنَّ تَكُونُونَ غُثَاءً كَغُثَاءِ السَّيْلِ ، يَنْتَزِعُ الْمَهَابَةَ مِنْ قُلُوبِ
عَدُوِّكُمْ ، وَيَجْعَلُ فِي قُلُوبِكُمُ الْوَهَنَ ، قَالَ : قُلْنَا : وَمَا الْوَهَنُ؟ قَالَ : حُبُّ
الْحَيَاةِ ، وَكَرَاهِيَةُ الْمَوْتِ

"The other nations are about to call one another in unity against you, just as those who are ready to eat unite on a container full of food." Someone asked, "Is it because we will be few at that time?" He replied, "No. Rather you will be many during that time, but you will be like the froth on flood waters. And Allāh will remove from the hearts of your enemies their fear of you, and He will place al-wahn in your hearts." He was asked, "And what is al-wahn, Messenger of Allāh?" He replied, "Love of this world and hatred of death."[232]

Ibn 'Umar narrated that he also said,

إِذَا تَبَايَعْتُمْ بِالْعِينَةِ وَأَخَذْتُمْ أَذْنَابَ الْبَقَرِ وَرَضِيتُمْ بِالزَّرْعِ وَتَرَكْتُمُ الْجِهَادَ ، سَلَّطَ
اللهُ عَلَيْكُمْ ذُلاًّ لاَ يَنْزِعُهُ حَتَّى تَرْجِعُوا إِلَى دِينِكُمْ

---

[232] *Sunan Abu Dawud*, vol. 3, p. 1196, no. 4284; authenticated in *Ṣaḥīḥ Sunan Abū Dāwūd*, vol. 3, p. 810, no. 3610.

"If you buy and sell using ʿīnah,[233] *and you takehold of the tails of cattle,*[234] *and agriculture becomes pleasing [i.e. sufficient] for you, and if you abandon jihād, then Allāh will cause a degradation to overcome you. And He will not remove it until you return to your religion."*[235]

Hence, the cure for this *Ummah's* countless diseases is correct faith and knowledge, and not the replacement of a particular regime. Furthermore, Muslims will not attain a position of true strength and honour until they fear Allāh and purify their practice of the religion from all *shirk*, innovation, and widespread corruption and heedlessness. Secondly, Muslims should be patient in giving *daʿwah*, constantly returning to Allāh and sincerely asking His guidance and aid. Because one's job is merely to convey, this does not imply that one is to convey the message only once, thus ending his or her responsibility. Nor does it mean that if a person does not accept one's *daʿwah* immediately, that person is a misguided deviant who should be avoided at all costs. Rather, a Muslim should display perseverance as well as gentleness in his *daʿwah* and take caution against labelling and name-calling others. Thirdly, Muslims should try their utmost to practise what they are preaching in their own daily lives, for Allāh says:

أَتَأْمُرُونَ ٱلنَّاسَ بِٱلْبِرِّ
وَتَنسَوْنَ أَنفُسَكُمْ وَأَنتُمْ تَتْلُونَ ٱلْكِتَٰبَ ۚ أَفَلَا تَعْقِلُونَ ﴿٤٤﴾

---

233 *ʿĪnah* is an interest-based loan masquerading as a business transaction. One person sells a commodity to another for a delayed payment. Then the original owner turns around and buys it back from the purchaser for cash at a lower price than he sold it for.

234 This is a reference to engagement in herding and farming at a time when *jihād* is necessary. *ʿAwn al-Maʿbūd*, vol. 9, p. 243.

235 *Sunan Abu Dawud*, vol. 2, pp. 985-6, no. 3455; authenticated in *Ṣaḥīḥ Sunan Abū Dāwūd*, vol. 2, p. 663, no. 2956; also collected by Aḥmad.

"Do you command people to righteousness and forget about your own selves, while you are [the ones] reciting the Scripture? Have you no sense?"

Sūrah al-Baqarah (2):44

Elsewhere, He states:

يَٰٓأَيُّهَا ٱلَّذِينَ ءَامَنُوا۟ لِمَ تَقُولُونَ مَا لَا تَفْعَلُونَ ۝٢
كَبُرَ مَقْتًا عِندَ ٱللَّهِ أَن تَقُولُوا۟ مَا لَا تَفْعَلُونَ ۝٣

"O believers, why do you say that which you do not do? Indeed it is most hateful in the sight of Allāh for you to say that which you do not do."

Sūrah al-Ṣaff (61):2-3

Since no human being is free of error, this does not mean that a Muslim must be perfect in order to give *da'wah*. He should, however, fear Allāh as much as he can in his daily life and steadily strive to attain a higher level of faith and righteous action, constantly repenting for his sins and working to correct them.

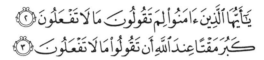

VERSE 27

فَلَمَّا رَأَوْهُ زُلْفَةً سِيٓـَٔتْ وُجُوهُ ٱلَّذِينَ كَفَرُوا۟ وَقِيلَ هَٰذَا ٱلَّذِى
كُنتُم بِهِۦ تَدَّعُونَ ﴿٢٧﴾

The faces of those who disbelieve will be gloomy, when they see it[236] approaching and they will be told: "This is what you were demanding!"

When the Day of Judgment is actually in sight and Hell is brought out, the disbelievers will realise that those whom they used to laugh at because of their faith were actually correct, and that they were terribly wrong. The realisation of their miscalculation will appear as horror and grief on their faces.

Their feelings of remorse and failure will be further intensified when the angels remind them that this was what they were defiantly demanding. Feelings of regret are at their height when a person cannot do anything to change the consequences of his or her actions. On the Day of Judgment, people cannot argue

[236] The torment on the Day of Resurrection.

their case, find excuses, run away, or beg for just one more chance. Allāh has already warned humankind of the terrifying regret and danger awaiting those who disobey Him and reject His message. He also warned them of the fact that on the Last Day, there will be no second chances. For example, He said:

وَٱتَّبِعُوٓا۟ أَحْسَنَ مَآ أُنزِلَ
إِلَيْكُم مِّن رَّبِّكُم مِّن قَبْلِ أَن يَأْتِيَكُمُ ٱلْعَذَابُ
بَغْتَةً وَأَنتُمْ لَا تَشْعُرُونَ ﴿٥٥﴾ أَن تَقُولَ نَفْسٌ يَٰحَسْرَتَىٰ
عَلَىٰ مَا فَرَّطتُ فِى جَنۢبِ ٱللَّهِ وَإِن كُنتُ لَمِنَ ٱلسَّٰخِرِينَ ﴿٥٦﴾
أَوْ تَقُولَ لَوْ أَنَّ ٱللَّهَ هَدَىٰنِى لَكُنتُ مِنَ ٱلْمُتَّقِينَ ﴿٥٧﴾
أَوْ تَقُولَ حِينَ تَرَى ٱلْعَذَابَ لَوْ أَنَّ لِى كَرَّةً فَأَكُونَ
مِنَ ٱلْمُحْسِنِينَ ﴿٥٨﴾

"Follow the best of that which is sent down to you from your Lord before the torment suddenly comes to you while you do not perceive it...or lest [a person] should say when he sees the torment, 'If only I had another chance [to return to the world], then I would certainly be among the doers of good!'"
Sūrah al-Zumar (39):55-8

Similarly, those who reject the Prophet's *Sunnah* will greatly regret it on the Day of Judgment. Allāh describes this scenario, saying:

وَيَوْمَ يَعَضُّ ٱلظَّالِمُ عَلَىٰ يَدَيْهِ يَقُولُ يَٰلَيْتَنِى ٱتَّخَذْتُ مَعَ
ٱلرَّسُولِ سَبِيلًا ﴿٢٧﴾ يَٰوَيْلَتَىٰ لَيْتَنِى لَمْ أَتَّخِذْ فُلَانًا خَلِيلًا ﴿٢٨﴾

"[On that] day, the oppressor will bite on his hands [from regret and fear] and say, 'If only I had taken the path with the Messenger! Ah! Woe to me! If only I had never taken so-and-so as a friend!'"

Sūrah al-Furqān (25):27-8

VERSE 28

قُلْ أَرَءَيْتُمْ إِنْ أَهْلَكَنِيَ ٱللَّهُ وَمَن مَّعِيَ أَوْ رَحِمَنَا فَمَن يُجِيرُ ٱلْكَٰفِرِينَ مِنْ عَذَابٍ أَلِيمٍ ﴿٢٨﴾

Say: "Tell me! Whether Allāh destroys me and those with me, or grants us His Mercy — who can save the disbelievers from a painful torment?"

The Prophet (ﷺ) and the believers down the ages are instructed to tell the disbelievers to save themselves, because nothing can save them from Allāh's punishment except sincere repentance and a return to Allāh's religion. Whatever ill that they wish to befall the believers will not benefit them. Whether Allāh punishes the believers or has mercy on them is all the same, relative to the disbelievers. There will be no escape from the torment of Hell for them.[237] After the time of Prophet Muḥammad (ﷺ),[238] when Allāh causes calamities to befall a

[237] *Tafsīr al-Qur'ān al-'Aẓīm*, vol. 4, p. 426.

[238] During the time of the Prophet (ﷺ), Allāh withheld punishment from the people as long as he remained among them. **"Allāh will not punish them while you [Muḥammad] are among them, nor will He punish them as long as they seek forgiveness."** (8:33)

people, they may also strike the righteous among them. He said:

وَٱتَّقُوا۟ فِتْنَةً لَّا تُصِيبَنَّ ٱلَّذِينَ ظَلَمُوا۟ مِنكُمْ خَآصَّةً ۖ وَٱعْلَمُوٓا۟ أَنَّ ٱللَّهَ شَدِيدُ ٱلْعِقَابِ ﴿٢٥﴾

"Fear the affliction which will not only affect those who do wrong, and know that Allāh is severe in punishment."
Sūrah al-Anfāl (8):25

Hence, Muslims living in the midst of disbelievers should make *hijrah* to Muslim lands to escape the punishments Allāh sends the disbelieving people.

Allāh's punishment may also befall the righteous if they are in the midst of corruption and do not command good and forbid evil. The Prophet (ﷺ) said,

مَا مِنْ قَوْمٍ يُعْمَلُ فِيهِمْ بِالْمَعَاصِي ثُمَّ يَقْدِرُونَ عَلَى أَنْ يُغَيِّرُوا ثُمَّ لَا يُغَيِّرُوا إِلَّا يُوشِكُ أَنْ يَعُمَّهُمُ اللَّهُ مِنْهُ بِعِقَابٍ

"There is no people among which evil is committed and they have the ability to change that but they do not change it, except that Allāh will soon afflict them with a punishment that will affect all of them."[239]

Commanding good and forbidding evil is a responsibility about which everyone will be questioned on the Day of Judgment. However, there are conditions attached to this noble act:[240]

---

[239] *Sunan Abu Dawud*, vol. 3, pp. 1207-8, no. 4324; authenticated in *Ṣaḥīḥ Sunan Abū Dāwūd*, vol. 3, p. 818, no. 3644. Also collected by al-Tirmidhī and Ibn Mājah.

[240] Much of the following information was taken primarily from Ibn Taymiyyah's *Essay on Commanding Good and Forbidding Evil* (English Translation), published by *al-Qur'an was-Sunnah Society of North America.*

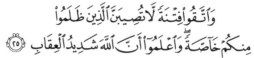

1) Capability - The level of obligation of a particular person is proportional to his or her capability, based on Allāh's statement: ***"Fear Allāh as much as you can."*** (64:16) In addition, the Prophet (ﷺ) said,

مَنْ رَأَى مِنكُمْ مُنْكَرًا فَلْيُغَيِّرْهُ بِيَدِهِ. فَإِنْ لَمْ يَسْتَطِعْ فَبِلِسَانِهِ. فَإِنْ لَمْ يَسْتَطِعْ فَبِقَلْبِهِ. وَذَلِكَ أَضْعَفُ الإِيمَانِ

"Whoever amongst you sees an evil must change it with his hand. If he is unable, let him change it with his tongue (i.e. speak out against it). If he is still unable, let him hate it in his heart, and that is the weakest level of faith."[241]

2) Security - One in a state of fear for his life or the lives of others is exempted from the obligation of commanding good and forbidding evil. This principle is deduced from the following *ḥadīth* of the Prophet (ﷺ):

إِنَّ اللهَ تَجَاوَزَ عَنْ أُمَّتِي الْخَطَأَ وَالنِّسْيَانَ، وَمَا اسْتُكْرِهُوا عَلَيْهِ

"Indeed Allāh has pardoned for my Ummah what they do out of error and forgetfulness, and what they were forced to do."[242]

3) Knowledge

الْقُضَاةُ ثَلَاثَةٌ: وَاحِدٌ فِي الْجَنَّةِ وَاثْنَانِ فِي النَّارِ، فَأَمَّا الَّذِي فِي الْجَنَّةِ فَرَجُلٌ عَرَفَ الْحَقَّ فَقَضَى بِهِ، وَرَجُلٌ عَرَفَ الْحَقَّ فَجَارَ فِي الْحُكْمِ فَهُوَ فِي النَّارِ وَرَجُلٌ قَضَى لِلنَّاسِ عَلَى جَهْلٍ فَهُوَ فِي النَّارِ

---

[241] *Sahih Muslim*, vol. 1, p. 33, no. 79.

[242] *Sunan Ibn Majah*, vol. 3, pp. 230-1, nos. 2043-5; authenticated by al-Albānī in *Ṣaḥīḥ al-Jāmiʿ al-Ṣaghīr*, vol. 1, p. 358, 1731.

"There are three types of judges. One will be in Paradise and the other two in Hell. A judge who knows the truth and rules by it will be in Paradise. One who knows the truth but is unjust in his rulings will be in the Fire, and one who is ignorant and judges between people will be in the Fire."[243]

Ibn Taymiyyah wrote the following concerning the importance of knowledge with regard to command: "Allāh ordered us to command good and forbid evil. However, in order to command something, it must first be known. One who does not know what is good cannot command that it be done. Likewise, in order to prohibit evil, it must first be known; for one who does not know what is evil cannot prohibit it."[244]

In addition, the methodology of commanding good and forbidding evil may be summarised as follows:

1) Gentleness - The way in which advice or instructions are given can often determine whether it will be accepted or not. Consequently, the use of gentle language is of utmost importance, as indicated in Allāh's command to Prophets Moses and Aaron when they were sent to Pharaoh:

اذْهَبَا إِلَىٰ فِرْعَوْنَ إِنَّهُ طَغَىٰ ﴿٤٣﴾ فَقُولَا لَهُ قَوْلًا لَّيِّنًا
لَّعَلَّهُ يَتَذَكَّرُ أَوْ يَخْشَىٰ ﴿٤٤﴾

"Go to Pharaoh for indeed he has transgressed. And speak to him mildly, perhaps he may accept admonition or fear [Allāh]."
Sūrah Ṭā Hā (20):43-4

---

[243] *Sunan Abu Dawud*, vol. 3, p. 1013, no. 3566; authenticated in *Ṣaḥīḥ Sunan Abū Dāwūd*, vol. 2, p. 682, no. 3051. Also collected by al-Tirmidhī and Ibn Mājah with slightly different wordings.

[244] *Majmūʿ al-Fatāwā*, vol. 15, p. 337.

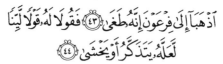

The Prophet (ﷺ) was also reported to have said,

إِنَّ اللهَ رَفِيقٌ يُحِبُّ الرِّفْقَ . وَيُعْطِي عَلَى الرِّفْقِ مَا لاَ يُعْطِي عَلَى الْعُنْفِ

"Indeed Allāh is gentle; He loves gentleness in all matters. He gives through gentleness what He does not give through harshness."[245]

And on another occasion he stated,

إِنَّ الرِّفْقَ لاَ يَكُونُ فِي شَيْءٍ إِلاَّ زَانَهُ ، وَلاَ يُنْزَعُ مِنْ شَيْءٍ إِلاَّ شَانَهُ

"Gentleness beautifies everything in which it exists, and harshness makes defective everything in which it exists."[246]

2) Patience - To effectively command good and forbid evil, patience is required since the response may often be rejection, abuse and/or physical attack. Allāh affirmed this principle by saying:

وَأْمُرْ بِالْمَعْرُوفِ وَانْهَ عَنِ الْمُنكَرِ وَاصْبِرْ عَلَىٰ مَا أَصَابَكَ إِنَّ ذَٰلِكَ مِنْ عَزْمِ الْأُمُورِ ﴿١٧﴾

"Command good and forbid evil, and be patient with whatever harm befalls you [as a result]. Indeed, that is the firmness [required for] matters."
Sūrah Luqmān (31):17

3) Moderation - It is essential that the limits set by Allāh be maintained without going to extremes in harshness or gentleness. In this regard, Ibn Taymiyyah wrote: "When

---

[245] *Sahih Muslim*, vol. 1, p. 1370, no. 6273.

[246] Ibid., no. 6274.

confronting sinful people, one should not exceed the limits of the *Sharī'ah* (law) in hating, prohibiting, abandoning, or punishing them. If one does so, he should be told to be concerned about himself. Those misguided cannot harm him if he is truly guided. Allāh stated, ***'O believers! Take care of your own selves. Those who are misguided cannot harm you if you are guided...'*** (5:105)."[247]

4) **Priority** - The goal of commanding good and forbidding evil is to achieve the greater good. Therefore, it is necessary to weigh the benefit and harm likely to result from commanding good and prohibiting evil. Ibn Taymiyyah commented on this principle as follows: "Commanding something good should not result in the loss of a greater good, or cause a greater evil. Likewise, forbidding something evil should not cause a greater evil or the loss of a greater good."[248] In addition, Ibn al-Qayyim said, "The Prophet (ﷺ) obliged his followers to forbid evil in order that the good loved by Allāh and His Messenger (ﷺ) will prevail. Consequently, if forbidding evil leads to what is worse and more hated by Allāh and His Messenger, it is prohibited to forbid it, even though Allāh hates evil and those who do it. For example, rebuking kings and rulers by rebelling and fighting against them is the foundation of evil and trials until the Last Day. The Companions sought the permission of Allāh's Messenger (ﷺ) to fight against their leaders whom he (ﷺ) foretold would delay prayer beyond its time. He replied, '*Not as long as they establish the prayer.*'[249] If one reflects on many trials and tribulations, great and small, which have occurred among Muslims, one would find that they resulted from the principle of not patiently dealing with evil, but rather, attempting to stop it irrationally, thereby causing greater

---

[247] *Majmū' al-Fatāwā*, vol. 14, pp. 381-97.

[248] *Al-Ḥisbah*, p. 124.

[249] *Sahih Muslim*, vol. 3, p. 1033, no. 4573.

evil. Allāh's Messenger (ﷺ) saw the greatest evils in Makkah without being able to change them (prior to the *Hijrah*)."[250]

There are several modern day examples of the impatience described above and its resulting harm. In Egypt, the so-called "*jihād*" group's execution of Sadāt brought a harsher ruler and greater repression. The Ikhwān uprising in Ḥams and Ḥamā in Syria led to the levelling of these towns, as well as the raping of hundreds of Muslim women by the Nuṣayrī regime of Hafiz al-Asad. In addition, the armed resistance of the F.I.S. in Algeria against the secular military rulers led to the mass slaughters of civilians by the G.I.A. and the discrediting of the Islamic movement. A similar case may be raised regarding Kashmir, where a revolt against Indian rule has led to the loss of thousands of Muslim lives over the past ten years, yet the movement is no closer to the goal than when it started. In fact, some of the leading factions have declared a unilateral cease-fire and are entering into negotiations with the Hindu government.

[250] *I'lām al-Muwaqqi'īn*, vol. 3, p. 4.

VERSE 29

قُلْ هُوَ
ٱلرَّحْمَٰنُ ءَامَنَّا بِهِۦ وَعَلَيْهِ تَوَكَّلْنَا فَسَتَعْلَمُونَ مَنْ هُوَ فِى ضَلَٰلٍ مُّبِينٍ

Say: "He is the Most Gracious. We believe in Him, and we put our trust in Him. You will soon come to know which of us is in obvious error."

True patience is the product of complete trust in Allāh at the time of calamity. Trust in one's Lord is an important aspect of worship and the natural consequence of real faith. Since belief in Allāh means accepting that nothing takes place in the universe without His permission, then only Allāh deserves humankind's complete trust. For it is only Allāh's promise which is never broken. No matter how righteous a human being may be, he or she is capable of error. Humans will always let each other down due to their erring nature. Consequently, Allāh quotes Prophet Jacob in chapter *Yūsuf* as saying:

إِنِ ٱلْحُكْمُ إِلَّا
لِلَّهِ ۖ عَلَيْهِ تَوَكَّلْتُ ۖ وَعَلَيْهِ فَلْيَتَوَكَّلِ ٱلْمُتَوَكِّلُونَ ﴿٦٧﴾

"The decision rests only with Allāh. I put my trust in Him alone and all who trust should only trust in Him."
Sūrah Yūsuf (12):67

Allāh further assures humankind that if they put their complete trust in Him, He will be sufficient for them in their most trying times.

وَمَن يَتَوَكَّلْ عَلَى ٱللَّهِ فَهُوَ حَسْبُهُۥٓ ۚ

"Whoever trusts in Allāh will find Him sufficient."
Sūrah al-Ṭalāq (65):3

Trust in Allāh is embodied in the firm belief that Allāh alone knows what is best for humankind; firm belief that what humans may perceive as being good for them may not, in the long run, be good for them. As Allāh said in *Sūrah al-Baqarah*:

وَعَسَىٰٓ أَن تَكْرَهُوا۟ شَيْـًٔا وَهُوَ خَيْرٌ لَّكُمْ ۖ وَعَسَىٰٓ أَن تُحِبُّوا۟
شَيْـًٔا وَهُوَ شَرٌّ لَّكُمْ ۗ وَٱللَّهُ يَعْلَمُ وَأَنتُمْ لَا تَعْلَمُونَ ﴿٢١٦﴾

"Perhaps you may dislike something and it is good for you, and you may like something and it is bad for you. Allāh knows and you do not."
Sūrah al-Baqarah (2):216[251]

---

[251] *The Purpose of Creation*, pp. 79-86.

Trust in Allāh also means that reliance on other than Allāh is, in fact, reliance on people or things that can neither benefit nor harm anyone. Thus, charms and amulets commonly used to attract good fortune and avert misfortune are all false. Use of such objects is a form of idolatry (*shirk*). Among Muslims of the Subcontinent, such charms are called '*tawīz*'[252] and in Sudan they are called '*hijāb*'.[253] Those who produce them utilise Qur'ānic verses reduced to numbers, according to the *Abjad* system of numerology.[254]

Numerology has no place in Islām. It was neither sanctioned by the Qur'ān nor by the Prophet Muḥammad (ﷺ) and was opposed by the Companions of the Prophet (ﷺ) as well as the early scholars. The great 14th century CE scholar Ibn Ḥajar al-ʿAsqalānī said, "[Numerology] is completely false and should not be relied on, for it has been accurately reported that the Companion of the Prophet (ﷺ) Ibn ʿAbbās used to forbid use of the *Abjad* and consider it a form of magic—which is quite reasonable, as it has no basis in the *Sharīʿah* (Islamic Law)."[255]

The origins of numerology can be found in the pagan beliefs of the ancient Babylonians and Greeks. Among the Assyrians and Babylonians, heavenly bodies were, at the same time, both deities and personified numbers. The star which they called *Ishtar* was both the goddess *Ishtar* and the deified number 15. The moon was not only earth's satellite, but also the lunar deity *Sin* and the deified number 30.[256] In

---

[252] This is the common pronunciation in the Urdu language. However, the correct Arabic pronunciation is *taʿwīdh*.

[253] *The Exorcist Tradition in Islaam*, pp. 308-9.

[254] *Abjad* is a system of calculation based on the correspondence of each letter of the Arabic alphabet with a number. (*The Concise Encyclopedia of Islam*, p. 16). This system was used by fortunetellers to interpret their clients' characters and predict the future. (*The Qur'an's Numerical Miracle: Hoax and Heresy*, p. 48)

[255] *Mabāḥith fī ʿUlūm al-Qur'ān*, pp. 237-8.

[256] *The New Encyclopedia Britannica*, vol. 12, p. 917.

Greece, the base can be found in the Pythagorean idea that all things can be expressed in numerical terms because they are ultimately reducible to numbers. Hence, in the Greek alphabet, each letter represented a number.[257] These ideas became incorporated in Judaism's esoteric branch known as the *Cabala*,[258] which is believed to date back at least to the time of Christ. The *Cabala* includes a numerological system called *gematria*, in which each letter of the Hebrew alphabet is given a numerical value and through which all kinds of mystic interpretations of the Scriptures can be made.[259] From Jewish mysticism, Greek philosophy and pagan Babylonian beliefs, Christian numerology evolved in the centres of learning in Alexandria and Syria. It later came into Arabia from Iraq and Syria along with the skill of writing. It is worth noting that the *Abjad* is in the order of the old Hebrew alphabet as far as 400, the six remaining letters being added by the Arabs.[260] However, the mathematical arrangement of the alphabet (the *Abjad*) was not used as numerals for counting, but was used by fortune-tellers to interpret their clients' characters and to divine the future, which explains why the Companion Ibn ʿAbbās did not hesitate in labelling it as a branch of magic. According to Islamic law, fortunetelling is included under the general heading of magic, which is itself classified as *ḥarām* (forbidden).[261]

There is a book called *Prophetic Medical Sciences*, published in India, which contains details of how to prepare amulets (*Tawīz*) in Part II, *Āina-e-Amaliyat* by Sufi Mohammad Azizur Rehman Sahib (Panipati) and in Part III, *Naqsh-e-Sulaimani* by Khuwaja Ashraf Ali Lucknowi. In Part II the contents

---

[257] *The New Encyclopedia Britannica*, vol. 7, p. 441.

[258] Literally "tradition or hidden wisdom".

[259] *Into The Unknown*, p. 63.

[260] *A Dictionary of Islam*, p. 3.

[261] *The Qur'an's Numerical Miracle*, pp. 47-8.

promise that amulets cause love, victory, pregnancy, increase sales in one's shop, and bring about the repayment of loans. It also promises that amulets can spoil bewitchment, release captives, return a run-away person, realign a displaced navel, and develop a strong memory. Among the important rules the author states are, Rule 3: Keeping in mind the position of the stars and moments is but essential for one who practises spells or writes an amulet, and Rule 5: Performing ablution is essential for muttering a spell or writing an amulet.[262]

Under the heading of "Miscellaneous [Amulets] For Love", the author writes:

> The following Naqsh (chart) is based on the following Ayat:[263]
>
> يُحِبُّونَهُم كَحُبِّ اللهِ وَالَّذِينَ آمَنُوا أَشَدُّ حُبًّا لِلهِ
>
> 786
>
> | | | | |
> |---|---|---|---|
> | 373 | 376 | 379 | 365 |
> | 378 | 366 | 372 | 377 |
> | 367 | 381 | 374 | 371 |
> | 375 | 370 | 368 | 380 |
>
> الحب فلان بن فلان على حبّ فلان بن فلان
>
> The woman who keeps this chart (Naqsh) with her shall be exceedingly loved by her husband and whoever looks at her will deeply love her.[264]

---

[262] *Prophetic Medical Sciences*, Part II, p. 4.

[263] ***"... They love them as they should only love Allāh. But the believers have a greater love for Allāh ..."*** It is a part of verse 165 of *Sūrah al-Baqarah*.

[264] *Prophetic Medical Sciences*, Part II, p. 10.

It is quite evident that these so-called 'Islamic' amulets are a mixture of Qur'ānic texts and pagan rites. The claims are themselves preposterous and the rules mix ablution (normally done for prayer) with astrology — which the Prophet (ﷺ) classified as a branch of magic, saying,

مَنِ اقْتَبَسَ عِلْمًا مِنَ النُّجُومِ اقْتَبَسَ شُعْبَةً مِنَ السِّحْرِ زَادَ مَا زَادَ

"Whoever acquires knowledge of any branch of astrology, has acquired knowledge of a branch of magic. The more he increases in that knowledge, the more he increases in sin."[265]

Such amulets also involve fortunetelling because those who prepare them claim knowledge of future events which will result from wearing these preparations. The Prophet (ﷺ) said,

مَنْ أَتَى كَاهِنًا فَصَدَّقَهُ بِمَا يَقُولُ فَقَدْ بَرِيءَ مِمَّا أُنْزِلَ عَلَى مُحَمَّدٍ صَلَّى اللّٰهُ عَلَيْهِ وَسَلَّمَ

"Whoever approaches a fortune-teller and believes what he says, has disbelieved in what was revealed to Muḥammad."[266]

The number at the top of the amulet '786' is commonly used in the Indian Subcontinent to indicate the phrase '*bismillāhir raḥmānir raḥīm*' [In the Name of Allāh, the Gracious, the Ever-Merciful]. It is derived from the *Abjad* system borrowed from Jewish mysticism, as previously mentioned. However, it could also represent many other statements of disbelief like 'Allāh is

---

[265] *Sunan Abu Dawud*, vol. 3, p. 1095, no. 3896; authenticated in *Ṣaḥīḥ Sunan Abū Dāwūd*, vol. 2, p. 739, no. 3305.

[266] *Sunan Abu Dawud*, vol. 3, p. 1095, no. 3895; authenticated in *Ṣaḥīḥ Sunan Abū Dāwūd*, vol. 2, p. 739, no. 3304.

not God and He is neither Gracious nor Merciful' or 'In the Name of Satan, the true God, Most Gracious'. Likewise, the remaining numbers in the chart, according to the *Abjad* could have many un-Islamic meanings.

Part III, *Naqsh-e-Sulaimani* contains similar amulets and prescriptions with even more elaborate charts and more outrageous claims. It also utilises astrology for determining the auspicious and inauspicious times for preparing amulets.

The author states:

> For making someone confess love, 'Bismillah' should be recited seven hundred and eighty-six times and after blowing over water, it should be given [to] the person concerned to drink, [and] the person will fall madly in love.[267]

Also:

> For love - The following should be burnt for three nights and the lamp should face the house of the beloved.

هھور. III ططط III III

ک

الحب فلان بن فلان على حب فلان بن فلان

Part IV of the book is called *Amal-e-Qur'ani* and is written by Maulana Ashraf Ali Sahib Thanvi. In it, the author makes the same outrageous claims as the previous sections. However, instead of using charts and numbers, he prescribes verses or parts of verses to be read along with certain unsanctioned acts.

---

[267] *Prophetic Medical Sciences*, Part III, p. 15.

For example, under the caption "MALE ISSUE", the author writes:

(1) Suratul Aala (P.30).
PROPERTY - The following Surah if written on the right rib of the woman in the offing[268] of pregnancy; then she will give birth to a son.

(2) If there is a woman who has not given birth to a son, saving female issues, then before passing out of three months of pregnancy write the following Ayat on the skin of the deer with saffron and rose water and make a tablet and tie it to the pregnant woman.

Ayat:[269]

ٱللَّهُ يَعۡلَمُ مَا تَحۡمِلُ كُلُّ أُنثَىٰ وَمَا تَغِيضُ ٱلۡأَرۡحَامُ
وَمَا تَزۡدَادُۖ وَكُلُّ شَيۡءٍ عِندَهُۥ بِمِقۡدَارٍ ۝٨

Then this Ayat:[270]

عَٰلِمُ ٱلۡغَيۡبِ وَٱلشَّهَٰدَةِ ٱلۡكَبِيرُ ٱلۡمُتَعَالِ ۝٩

(3) And the reliable source has also given to know that the woman who does not beget a male child do the following. "Draw a circle on her abdomen and by the tip of your finger complete 70 rounds of the circle by saying "Ya Mateeno."
The purpose will be served.

---

[268] i.e., the beginning

[269] Sūrah al-Ra'd (13):8. *"Allāh knows what every female bears, and by how much the wombs fall short or exceed. Everything with Him is in proportion."*

[270] The following verse (13):9: *"Knower of the unseen and the seen, the Most Great, the Most High."*

(4) If "Surah Yusuf" is written on a piece of paper and tied on a pregnant woman she will beget a male child.[271]

Such claims have no basis in the *Sunnah*. Prophet Muḥammad (ﷺ) was not recorded, even in inauthentic narrations of *ḥadīth*, to have made such pronouncements. At most, it can be said that the last two chapters of the Qur'ān were revealed when the Prophet (ﷺ) was suffering from a magical spell and that he instructed 'Alī to recite them over himself and the spell was broken.[272] It is also reported that some Companions of the Prophet (ﷺ) recited *Sūrah al-Fātiḥah* over a person who was possessed and he was cured. After doing that, the Companion informed the Prophet (ﷺ) and got his approval.[273] No one has the authority to make claims like those mentioned above. The Qur'ān is not a medicine book which 'spiritual' doctors can pick and choose from to cause love and male children. Whatever Prophet Muḥammad (ﷺ) prescribed was based on divine revelation which ceased with his death. Furthermore, Allāh clearly stated that the religion was complete with the Prophet (ﷺ): ***"Today I have completed your religion for you."***[274] And Imām Mālik ibn Anas was reported to have said that whatever was not a part of the religion when that verse was revealed, can never be a part of the religion.

Allāh concludes this verse by quoting the believers, reminding the disbelievers that one day soon they will realise who the misguided ones really are. In this life, both "Muslims" and non-Muslims attack the true believers, who are striving to

---

[271] *Prophetic Medical Sciences*, Part IV, pp. 29-30.

[272] *Sahih Al-Bukhari*, vol. 7, pp. 443-4, no. 660; and *Sahih Muslim*, vol. 3, pp. 1192-3, no. 5428.

[273] *Sunan Abu Dawud*, vol. 3, p. 1092, no. 3887; authenticated in *Ṣaḥīḥ Sunan Abū Dāwūd*, vol. 2, p. 737, no. 3297.

[274] *Sūrah al-Mā'idah* (5):3.

practise Islām as completely as possible, mocking them and calling them "extremists", "fanatics", "crazy", etc. Allāh describes this reality as follows:

إِنَّ ٱلَّذِينَ
أَجْرَمُوا۟ كَانُوا۟ مِنَ ٱلَّذِينَ ءَامَنُوا۟ يَضْحَكُونَ ﴿٢٩﴾ وَإِذَا مَرُّوا۟ بِهِمْ
يَتَغَامَزُونَ ﴿٣٠﴾ وَإِذَا ٱنقَلَبُوٓا۟ إِلَىٰٓ أَهْلِهِمُ ٱنقَلَبُوا۟ فَكِهِينَ ﴿٣١﴾
وَإِذَا رَأَوْهُمْ قَالُوٓا۟ إِنَّ هَٰٓؤُلَآءِ لَضَآلُّونَ ﴿٣٢﴾ وَمَآ أُرْسِلُوا۟ عَلَيْهِمْ
حَٰفِظِينَ ﴿٣٣﴾

"Indeed the criminals used to laugh at the believers; and whenever they passed them by, they winked to each other [in mockery]. And when they returned to their own people, they would return jesting. And whenever they saw them, they said, 'These [people] have certainly gone astray!' But they [the disbelievers] have not been sent to watch over them."

Sūrah al-Muṭaffifīn (83):29-33

However, Allāh then reassures the believers that on the Day of Resurrection, the tables will be turned. He goes on to say:

فَٱلْيَوْمَ ٱلَّذِينَ ءَامَنُوا۟ مِنَ ٱلْكُفَّارِ يَضْحَكُونَ ﴿٣٤﴾ عَلَى ٱلْأَرَآئِكِ
يَنظُرُونَ ﴿٣٥﴾ هَلْ ثُوِّبَ ٱلْكُفَّارُ مَا كَانُوا۟ يَفْعَلُونَ ﴿٣٦﴾

"But this Day [the Day of Judgment] the believers will laugh at the disbelievers, [as they sit] on high thrones, looking around. So aren't the disbelievers fully paid for what they used to do?"

Sūrah al-Muṭaffifīn (83):34-6

VERSE 30 قُلْ أَرَءَيْتُمْ إِنْ أَصْبَحَ مَآؤُكُمْ غَوْرًا فَمَن يَأْتِيكُم بِمَآءٍ مَّعِينٍۢ ﴿٣٠﴾

Say: "Tell me! Who could supply you with flowing water if your water were to sink [back in the ground]?"

The chapter closes with a parable taken from a reality of the physical world. If one day all the springs, wells and rivers dried up, human existence as well as that of all living creatures would be threatened with extinction. Human beings are not able to create springs or dig wells anywhere. Instead they collect the spring waters in wells, reservoirs, and dams. Then they harness hydroelectric power through turbines and use its waters through irrigation. It is a mercy from Allāh that He has caused water to spring forth from the bowels of the earth and caused it to flow in all regions of the earth according to human need.[275] Elsewhere in the Qur'ān, Allāh says:

---

[275] *Tafsīr al-Qur'ān al-'Aẓīm*, vol. 4, p. 426.

أَفَرَءَيْتُمُ ٱلْمَآءَ ٱلَّذِى تَشْرَبُونَ ﴿٦٨﴾ ءَأَنتُمْ أَنزَلْتُمُوهُ مِنَ ٱلْمُزْنِ
أَمْ نَحْنُ ٱلْمُنزِلُونَ ﴿٦٩﴾ لَوْ نَشَآءُ جَعَلْنَٰهُ أُجَاجًا فَلَوْلَا تَشْكُرُونَ

"Tell me! The water that you drink: is it you who cause it to come down from the clouds, or am I the one who causes it to come down? If I had willed, I could have certainly made it salty [and undrinkable]. So why then do you not thank Allāh?"

Sūrah al-Wāqi'ah (56):68-70

APPENDIX

The following is a list of common inauthentic *ḥadīths* regarding *Sūrah al-Mulk*.[276]

> 1. *Ibn ʿAbbās reported that one of the Prophet's Companions set up a tent on a grave without realising it was a grave. There suddenly appeared a person in the tent reciting Sūrah "Tabārakal-ladhī biyadihil-mulk" to its end. The Companion went to the Messenger of Allāh (ﷺ) and said, "Messenger of Allāh, I set up my tent on a grave without realising it, and a man appeared reciting Sūrah Tabārak until its end!" Allāh's Messenger (ﷺ) replied, "It is al-Māniʿah (the Preventer), it is al-Munajjiyah (the Saviour), providing salvation from the punishment of the grave."*
>
> Collected by al-Tirmidhī and declared inauthentic in *Ḍaʿīf Sunan al-Tirmidhī*, p. 345, no. 546.
>
> 2. *Ibn ʿAbbās quoted Allāh's Messenger (ﷺ) as saying, "I wish that it was in the heart of every believer." That is, Tabārakal-ladhī biyadihil-mulk.*

[276] This list was taken from *al-Fulk fī Faḍl Sūratul-Mulk*, by Abū ʿAbdur-Raḥmān Fawzī ibn ʿAbdillāh ibn Muḥammad.

Collected by al-Bayhaqī in *Shuʿab al-Īmān*, vol. 5, p. 446, and declared inauthentic in *Ḍaʿīf al-Jāmiʿ al-Ṣaghīr*, p. 883.

3. *Anas ibn Mālik related that Allāh's Messenger (ﷺ) said, "Indeed a man from before your time died without having anything from Allāh's Book except Tabārak. When he was placed in his grave the Angel came to him and the Sūrah flared up in its face. The Angel told it, 'Certainly you are from Allāh's Book and I dislike causing you any harm. I do not have the power to harm or benefit either you or the man. So if you wish to protect him, go to the Lord and tell him, 'O Lord, indeed so-and-so chose me from Your Book and learned me and recited me. Will You burn him with the Fire and punish him while I am inside him? If You are going to do that then erase me from Your Book.' When He says, 'Am I seeing you angry?' tell Him, 'It is my right to be angry.' He will say, 'Go, for I have given him to you. Welcome to that mouth, perhaps it recited Me; welcome to that chest, perhaps it stored me; welcome to those feet, perhaps they stood up in prayer for Me. Keep his company in his grave to prevent him from feeling loneliness.'" When Allāh's Messenger (ﷺ) related this, every child, elder, freeman and slave learned it and Allāh's Messenger (ﷺ) called it al-Munajjiyah."*

Collected by Ibn ʿAsākir in *Tārīkh* according to Ibn Kathīr, who stated that it was very inauthentic.

4. *Anas ibn Nufayl related that the Prophet (ﷺ) said, "A man will be resurrected on the Day of Judgment who did all possible sins, except that*

he used to maintain the unity of Allāh, and he only used to read one chapter from the Qur'ān. It will be ordered that he be taken to the Hellfire and something like a comet will fly out from his insides saying, 'O Allāh, I am from what You revealed to Your Prophet and this slave of Yours used to recite me.' And it will continue to intercede until it gets him into paradise. It is al-Munajjiyah: Tabārakal-ladhī bi yadihil-mulk."

Collected by al-Daylamī in *al-Firdaws*, vol. 5, p. 467. Saʿīd ibn Maslamah is in its chain of narration and he is unreliable according to *al-Taqrīb* (p. 241).

5. *Ibn 'Abbās narrated that Allāh's Messenger (ﷺ) said, "Certainly I find in Allāh's Book a chapter of thirty verses; whoever recites it at the time of sleep will have thirty good deeds recorded for him, thirty evil deeds erased and he will be raised by thirty degrees. And Allāh will send an angel to him to spread its wing over him and protect him from every evil until he awakens. It is al-Mujādilah (The Arguer). It will argue for its companion in the grave. It is Tabārakal-ladhī bi yadihil-mulk."*

Collected by al-Daylamī in *al-Firdaws*, vol. 1, p. 62-3, and its chain of narrators was declared extremely weak by al-Suyūṭī in *al-Durr al-Manthūr*, vol.6, p. 247.

6. *Anas stated that the Prophet (ﷺ) said, "I saw something amazing! I saw a man who died having many sins and who squandered his wealth. But when punishment was sent to him in his grave and directed at his feet or his head,*

the chapter which has in it the bird, argued with the punishment on his behalf, saying, 'He used to guard me and my Lord promised me that whoever continuously recites me will not be punished.' It turned the punishment away from him." Anas further said that the Muslim emigrants and those from Madīnah used to learn it and they used to say that one who did not learn Sūrah al-Mulk was cheated.

Collected by al-Suyūṭī in *al-Durr al-Manthūr*, vol. 6, p. 247 who declared it an unreliable narration from al-Daylamī.

7. Anas was also reported to have quoted Allāh's Messenger (ﷺ) as saying, "There is a chapter in the Qur'ān which will intercede on behalf of its companion and put him in paradise. It is Tabārakal-ladhī bi yadihil-mulk wa huwa 'alā kulli shay'in qadīr."

Collected by Ibn 'Abdul-Barr in *al-Tamhīd*, vol. 7, p. 261-2, and is inauthentic due to two of the narrators being unknown and one unreliable.[277]

---

[277] See *al-Fulk fī Faḍl Sūratul-Mulk*, p. 68-69.

BIBLIOGRAPHY

Abbasi, S.M. Madani.
Riyaḍ al-Ṣāliḥīn.
Beirut: Dār Al Arabia, n.d.

Albānī, Muḥammad Nāṣir Uddīn al-.
Ṣaḥīḥ al-Jāmiʿ al-Ṣaghīr.
Beirut: al-Maktab al-Islāmī, 3rd ed., 1990.

…………………,
Ṣaḥīḥ Sunan Abū Dāwūd.
Beirut: al-Maktab al-Islāmī, 1st ed., 1989.

…………………,
Ṣaḥīḥ Sunan al-Tirmidhī.
Beirut: al-Maktab al-Islāmī, 1st ed., 1988.

…………………,
Ṣaḥīḥ Sunan Ibn Mājah.
Beirut: al-Maktab al-Islāmī, 3rd ed., 1988.

Albar, Mohammed Ali.
Human Development.
Jeddah: Saudi Publishing & Distributing House, 3rd ed., 1992.

'Alī, Ibrāhīm al-.
Ṣaḥīḥ al-Sīrah al-Nabawiyyah.
Amman: Dār al-Nafā'is, 1st ed. 1995.

Ali, Abdullah Yusuf.
The Holy Qur'an, English translation of the meanings and Commentary.
Al-Madīnah: King Fahd Holy Qur'an Printing Complex, Dār al-Iftā revision, 1990.

Anbari, Khalid al-'.
The Fundamentals of Takfir.
Detroit: Al-Qur'an was-Sunnah Society of North America, 1999.

Arberry, Arthur J.
The Koran Interpreted.
London: Gorge Allen & Unwin Publishers Ltd, 1955, 1980.

Asad, Muhammad.
The Message of The Qur'an.
London: E.J. Brill, 1st ed., 1980.

Bailey, Ron.
Into The Unknown.
USA: Readers Digest Assn. Inc., 1981.

Bucaille, Maurice.
Moses and Pharaoh: The hebrews in Egypt.
Rokyo: NRR Mediascope, 1st ed. 1994.

....................,
The Qur'ān and Modern Science.
Sharjah, UAE : Dar Al Fatah, 1996.

Dehlvi, Maulana Ahmad Saeed.
Prophetic Medical Sciences.
Karachi: Darul-Ishāt, 1989.

Fazal-ul-Karim, Al-Haj Maulana.
Al Hadis.
Karachi: Darul Ishāt, 1st ed., 1994.

....................,
Imam Gazzali's: Ihya 'Ulum-ud-Din.
Lahore: Kazi Publications, n.d.

Glasse, Cyril.
The Concise Encyclopaedia of Islam.
London: Stacey International, 1989.

Guillaume, A.
The Life of Muhammad: Translation of Ibn Ishaq's Sirah Rasul Allah.
Karachi: Oxford University Press, 6th ed., 1980.

Haddad and Smith, Yvonne Yazbeck and Jane Idleman.
Mission to America.
Florida: The University Press of Florida,1993.

Hughes, Thomas Patrick.
A Dictionary of Islam.
Lahore: Premier Book House, n.d.

Ibn Kathīr, Ismā'īl.
Tafsīr al-Qur'ān al-'Aẓīm.
Beirut: Dār al-Kutub al-'Ilmiyyah, 1986.

Kamali, Mohammad Hashim.
The Principles of Islamic Jurisprudence.
Cambridge: Islamic Texts Society, 1991.

Khalifa, Rashad.
Mu'jizah al-Qur'an al-Karim.
Tucson, Arizona: Masjid Tucson, 1980.

....................,
Quran: Visual Presentation of the Miracle.
Tuscon, Arizona: Islamic Productions, 1982.

Lane, E.W.
Arabic-English Lexicon.
Cambridge, England: Islamic Texts Society, 1984.

Maududi, S. Abul A'la.
The Meaning of the Qur'an.
Lahore: Islamic Publications Ltd., 4th ed., 1993.

Moore, Keith L., Abdul-Majīd Zindani and Mustafa Ahmed.
The Qur'an and Modern Science: Correlation Studies.
Makkah: Islamic Academy for Scientific Research, 1990.

Naik, Zakir.
Qur'an & Modern Science: Compatible or Incompatible.
Mumbai, India: Islamic Research Foundation, 2000.

Nawawī, Yaḥyā ibn Sharaf, al-.
Sharḥ al-Nawawī 'alā Ṣaḥīḥ Muslim.
Cairo: Dār Abū Ḥayyān.

Philips, Abu Ameenah Bilal.
Fundamentals of Tawheed.
Riyadh: Tawheed Publications, 1st ed., 1989.

....................,
Ibn Taymiyyah's Essay on the Jinn.
Riyadh: Tawheed Publications, 1st ed., 1989.

………………..,
The Exorcist Tradition in Islaam.
Sharjah, U.A.E.: Dar Al Fatah Press, 1st ed., 1997.

………………..,
The Purpose of Creation.
Sharjah, U.A.E.: Dar Al Fatah Press, 1st ed., 1995.

………………..,
The Qur'an's Numerical Miracle: Hoax and Heresy.
Jeddah, Saudi Arabia: Abul Qasim Bookstore, 1st ed., 1987.

………………..,
The True Message of Jesus Christ.
Sharjah, U.A.E.: Dar Al Fatah Press, 1st ed., 1996.

………………..,
Usool at-Tafseer.
Sharjah, U.A.E.: Dar al Fatah, 1997.

Qāsimī, Muḥammad Jamāluddīn al-.
Qawā'id al-Taḥdīth min Funūn Muṣṭalaḥ al-Ḥadīth.
Beirut: Dār al-Kutub al-'Ilmiyyah, n.d.

Qaṭṭān, Mannā'.
Mabāḥith fī 'Ulūm al-Qur'ān.
Riyadh: Maktabah al-Ma'ārif, 8th ed., 1981.

Robeson, James.
Mishkāt al-Maṣābīḥ.
Lahore: Sh. Muhammad Ashraf Publishers, 1975.

Ṣāliḥ, Subḥī.
Mabāḥith fī 'Ulūm al-Qur'ān.
Beirut: Dār al-'Ilm lil-Malāyīn, 14th ed., 1982.

Suyūṭī, ʻAbdul-Raḥmān al-.
Al-Itqān fī ʻUlūm al-Qur'ān.
Cairo: al-Ḥalabī Press, 4th ed., 1978

The New Encyclopedia Britannica.
USA: Encyclopedia Britannica Enc., 15th ed., 1985.